MW01094184

PROPHETIC PROTOCOLS & ETHICS

A Handbook for Accurate Prophetic Operations

by Jennifer LeClaire

Best-Selling Author of the Making of a Prophet

PROPHETIC PROTOCOLS & ETHICS
A HANDBOOK FOR ACCURATE PROPHETIC OPERATIONS
Copyright © Jennifer LeClaire 2020

Unless otherwise noted, Scripture quotations are taken from the Modern English Version of the Bible.

Jennifer LeClaire's books are available at most Christian bookstores.
Published by Awakening Media
P.O. Box 30563
Fort Lauderdale, FL 33301
www.jenniferleclaire.org

TABLE OF CONTENTS

i

1

WHAT ARE PROPHETIC PROTOCOLS & ETHICS?

Some prophets, seers and otherwise prophetic people have never heard of prophetic protocols. Others have functioned under an unction, unaware of the need for protocols that serve as banks on the prophetic rivers. Still others have operated almost instinctively in some, if not many or even all, of the protocols outlined in this book without anyone but the Holy Spirit leading, guiding and teaching them.

What are prophetic protocols and ethics? A protocol is a code prescribing strict adherence to correct etiquette and precedence, according to *Merriam-Webster*'s dictionary. A protocol outlines the correct way something should be done.

Prophetic protocols are established by the Word and Spirit of God, not by me or any man. Sure, some denominations may have established rigid and even ridiculous protocols for prophetic ministry that have given protocols a bad name. But the Bible does give us clear guidelines for operating in prophetic ministry and there is wisdom gained from experience.

Yes, there is a right way to operate in prophetic ministry. The right way blesses the Body of Christ through edification, exhortation, comfort, and at times direction and correction. Yes, there's more than one right way to operate in prophetic ministry, but there is a "right way." Again, we're not talking about man-made rules and regulations, rather Scriptures and Spirit-inspired wisdom gained through experience.

Of course, there is also a wrong way to operate in prophetic ministry. The wrong way brings harm to the Body through presumption, false operations, ill-timed prophetic words and the like. Indeed, there's more than one wrong way to operate in prophetic ministry, but there is a "wrong way." Most people who operate the "wrong way" do so innocently, because they haven't been exposed to the right way. No one has trained them. They haven't seen anybody else do it. They don't have a solid mentor.

Thankfully, that can easily be corrected by understanding guidelines like those in this book.

The Case for Prophetic Precedence

Consider this: The concept of "precedence" is part of the definition of protocols. Precedence is how things have been done, and the way things have worked in the past. When attorneys argue legal cases and when judges rule, they look to precedents to help guide them to a right decision. We have the Bible as a precedent, as well as the modern-day prophetic movement with its successes and missteps, to help us flow in godly prophetic operations.

Please understand, I'm not writing a rule book on protocols and ethics from a heart posture that I alone have all the answers on how things should be done, but it is helpful to have guidelines and standards.

I've walked in prophetic ministry now for decades. I've seen how much more fruitful prophetic ministry is when these protocols and ethics are exercised. The Holy Spirit may lead you to break some of the protocols listed in this book for various reasons, but it would that would be an exception in most cases.

Understanding Prophetic Ethics

Ethics are different than protocols. What are ethics? *Merriam-Webster's* dictionary defines ethics as, "the discipline dealing with what is good and bad and with moral duty and obligation; a set of moral principles : a theory or system of moral values, the principles of conduct governing an individual or a group, a guiding philosophy, a consciousness of moral importance."

Protocols, then, are the guidelines for safe and effective prophetic ministry. Ethics are the boundaries of what is right. Just because a method of prophetic ministry is effective doesn't make it ethical. You can get money from robbing a bank, that doesn't make it ethical. You can become a doctor by cheating on your exams, but that doesn't make it ethical. You can write a book by way of plagiarism, but that doesn't make it ethical.

Some of these protocols were taught to me. Others the Holy Spirit taught me directly through experience in prophetic ministry. Some of these protocols are what I would call always-dos. Some of the protocols are only necessary on rare occasion—but we need to be aware of them because when you are in the throes of prophetic ministry, you may not otherwise know what to do. This book will give you a heads up.

2

DO WE REALLY SO MANY PROPHETIC PROTOCOLS?

When you learn to drive a car, there are many operations you have to master before the government will let you legally on the road. There's also a thick book of traffic rules you have to memorize before they'll give you a license to drive on the streets so you don't crash.

Not so in prophetic ministry. Anyone who is filled with the Holy Spirit has a license to prophesy. The lack of training is why we sometimes see prophetic car crashes. Like Driver's Ed, we need Prophetic Ed. Anyone who supposes to speak in the name of the Lord should want to release His voice accurately in a way that helps not harms. That means understanding at least some basic protocols.

Think about it this way. Technically, someone could drive a car in any nation without understanding the protocols of the road or the functions of a vehicle. That driver may actually do fairly well driving down a straight road in the sunlight. But what happens when it gets dark or there is heavy traffic or they enter a highway where the speed limit doubles? What if it's raining? What if they don't understand what the green, yellow and red lights mean, or the danger of tailgating, or how to use the horn on the car?

Likewise, technically speaking, anyone can get a scalpel and make an incision in the area of the appendix, but if you don't understand how to do the surgery you're likely to cause someone great harm. Anyone can cut your hair, but you might not like the way it turns out.

You get the picture, right? Protocols and ethics are not meant to be religious rules, but boundaries that keep people, including you, safe. They are guidelines for safe prophetic operations for all parties involved. If we are serious about being a blessing with our prophetic ministry, we should be interested in doing something the right way.

Although I've been teaching prophetic protocols for many years, now is the time to issue a book with deeper teachings in the second wave of the prophetic. I sit on the Apostolic Council of Prophetic Elders, which Cindy Jacobs oversees. The Word of the Lord for 2020, compiled by Cindy after the meeting of the council, included these words:

"Now, I do want to say, I know we are not the only prophets; there are many groups of prophets. But our particular group that's met so long felt that we should give a cautionary word that we need to once again issue guidelines on prophesying, like not telling people who to marry, when to make a move and things like this, or saying "'thus saith the Lord' as you're just beginning. We need to be teaching these things again."

Prophetic Protocols Are in the Bible

Despite wisdom from prophetic elders, many people have balked at prophets who teach prophetic protocols. Some have accused prophets who teach these guidelines of quenching the Holy Spirit or being legalistic. Usually those voices are ones you wouldn't want prophesying to you. Teaching protocols and ethics is not legalism, it's wisdom.

Paul taught protocols for spiritual gifts in his Spirit-inspired writings. One of them is in 1 Corinthians 14:39-40: "Therefore, brothers, eagerly desire to prophesy, and do not forbid speaking in tongues. Let all things be done decently and in order."

God is a God of order. So while some want to criticize prophetic protocols, they are necessary because a reckless approach to prophetic ministry can do great damage to individual lives, churches and the Body of Christ as a whole. Indeed, many churches have banned and banished prophets and prophetic ministry because of irresponsible, unaccountable and even rebellious people who insist they are being led by the Spirit.

Unfortunately, some have thrown out the baby with the bathwater because of a bad experience. Prophetic ministry is invaluable to the Body of Christ. I've seen countless lives transformed by prophetic ministry done the right way. We want to represent God well.

God is not the author of confusion but of peace (see 1 Corinthians 14:33). Prophetic operations without protocol can often generate confusion, chaos and even shipwreck people's faith. Prophets are oracles and mouthpieces for God, yet some of what comes out of people's mouths in His name can be self-willed, self-promotional witchcraft. You can read more about that in my book, *Discerning Prophetic Witchcraft*. We must be willing to submit our prophetic ministry to elders for accountability, especially when the word may cause shock or stir people in the body to fear or confusion.

What About Prophetic Liberty?

Yes, where the Spirit of the Lord is, there is liberty (see 2 Corinthians 3:17) but we don't have to throw order out the window in the name of freedom. Freedom and order are not mutually exclusive concepts. It's not an either/or option. Consider this passage Paul wrote, inspired by the Spirit of God, from 1 Corinthians 14:27-31:

"If anyone speaks in an unknown tongue, let it be by two, or at the most by three, and each in turn, and let one interpret. But if there is no interpreter, let him remain silent in the church, and let him speak to himself and to God. Let two or three prophets speak, and let the others judge. If anything is revealed to another that sits by, let the first keep silent. For you may all prophesy one by one, that all may learn and all may be encouraged."

Can you see the order here? These verses also include an element of judging prophecy, which we'll discuss in the book. Accountability includes judging—or discerning the spirit behind—prophetic words. Prophecies released in a public setting over a congregation, especially, should be judged and if necessary, corrected, because wrong words can lead people in a wrong direction. We are responsible for the integrity of what we release and should have a healthy fear of the Lord on this front.

Prophets Need Self-Control
Some prophetic people reject any call for order or protocols, claiming they just can't help themselves—that they can't control what the Spirit does through them. This is concerning and violates Scripture on several levels. First, one of the fruits of the Spirit is self-control, according to Galatians 5:22-23. Second, the Bible says: "The spirits of the prophets are subject to the prophets" (1 Corinthians 14:32).

God can't make you open your mouth and pray or prophesy—well, He could but He typically doesn't. The Greek word for "subject" in that verse is *hupotasso*, which means to submit to one's control, to obey, to subordinate. The excuse that you "just can't help it" flies in the face of Scripture and order. We need to stop blaming our goofiness on the Holy Ghost!

3

HOW TO USE THIS BOOK

This book is meant to offer guidelines for safe and effective prophesy. It's not meant to restrain or constrain your prophetic flow or give you a rule book to criticize others in a legalistic spirit, or to lead you into the paralysis by analysis. This book aims to help you protect the integrity of your prophetic ministry by avoiding pitfalls others, even very reputable prophets, have fallen into headlong.

This book is meant to help you remember, in the heat of revival, some of what you already know, or teach you what to do in situations you've never been in before. I hope this book helps you come up higher in the way you handle prophecy and gain more confidence in what you release.

I would suggest reading the book through from beginning to end. The protocols are not outlined in any specific order of importance. They are all important, some are critical. This is not meant to be an exhaustive list. You may think of something practical I've left out, though it is very thorough.

You may need to read this over and over again to remember some of what you need to learn for various situations in which you find yourself. You might also find yourself referring back to it for yourself or to teach others. At the same time, depending on your level and frequency of prophetic ministry, some of these protocols may never apply to the type of utterances you release.

I am not Moses. I am not laying down a prophetic law. The spirit of this book is to help you rise up and be as accurate, diplomatic and Christlike as possible. Jesus is our prototype prophet. We should ultimately model our prophetic ministry after His. Beyond this helpful book on protocols, I urge you to study the prophetic ministry of Christ. You can pick up a copy of my book, *Christ the Prophet: Understanding Jesus' Prophetic Ministry.*

In personal prophecy situations, abide by the 1 Corinthians 4:3 mandate to edify, comfort and exhort. You've heard the saying, "Anyone can find the dirt in someone, so look for the gold." This sentiment is the foundation of New Testament prophetic ministry.

The Greek word for "edification" in 1 Corinthians 4:3 is "oikodomoe." According to *The KJV New Testament Greek Lexicon*, it means 1. (the act of) building up, building up; 2. edifying, edification, the act of one who promotes another's growth in Christian wisdom, piety, happiness and holiness.

Merriam-Webster's dictionary puts it plainly: edification is "an act or process of edifying." And edify means to build, establish, and instruct and improve especially in moral and religious knowledge. It also means to uplift, enlighten and inform. This is part of the purpose of the simple gift of prophecy.

The Greek word for "exhortation" in this verse is "paraklesis." According to *The KJV New Testament Greek Lexicon*, it means: 1. a calling near, summons; 2. importation, supplication and entreaty; 3. exhortation admonition and encouragement; 4. consolation, comfort, solace, that which affords comfort or refreshment; 5. persuasive discourse, stirring address, instructive, admonitory, conciliatory, powerful hortatory discourse.

Merriam-Webster defines exhortation as "the act or instance of exhorting; language intended to incite and encourage." Exhort means "to incite by argument or advice: urge strongly; to give warnings or advice, to make urgent appeals." Warnings are part of exhortation at the level the office of the prophet but the simple gift of prophecy does not go beyond the bounds of encouragement, inspiration and consolation. Of course, the Lord can use any believer to deliver a warning.

The Greek word for "comfort" in this verse is "paramuthia." According to the lexicon, the word means "any address, whether made for the purpose of persuading, or of arousing and stimulating or of calming and consoling; consolation, comfort."

Merriam-Webster defines comfort as "to give strength and hope to; to ease the grief or trouble of." Given the Holy Spirit is our Comforter, this is one of the easiest aspects of the simple gift of prophecy to understand.

Although there are times the Lord will inspire a prophet to speak forth a word of warning or even correction publicly, this is not the New Testament norm—especially without relationship. And this is not in the bounds of 1 Corinthians 4:3. The Lord's first instinct is not to embarrass people publicly, and people are not as likely to receive the word if they are embarrassed, even if it is valid.

That doesn't mean the Lord won't issue a public rebuke through a prophet, but this is rare and, again, it is not in the bounds of 1 Corinthians 4:3. That means prophetic believers should not default to this flow. Discretion is key when offering correction in the name of prophesy. (Remember, Nathan rebuked David privately). Exhortation is different than correction, but can feel like correction to someone who is insecure.

PROTOCOL 2
DO JUDGE YOUR REVELATION BEFORE RELEASING IT

When possible, you should judge your prophetic revelation before releasing it, especially if it is beyond the bounds of edification, exhortation and comfort.

Remember, judging your prophecy is first your responsibility. That means you need to learn the principles of testing the spirits. Before you take prophetic revelation to other people to judge—and before you release it publicly—take time to judge it yourself. Ensure the revelation is in line with Scripture and that you aren't filtering what you saw, heard or experienced through your own biases. Although you could still judge wrongly, you should make testing the spirit behind the prophetic revelation your first effort after reception.

1 John 4:1 exhorts believers: "Beloved, do not believe every spirit, but test the spirits, whether they are of God; because many false prophets have gone out into the world." *The Passion Translation* puts it this way: "Delightfully loved friends, don't trust every spirit, but carefully examine what they say to determine if they are of God, because many false prophets have mingled into the world."

This verse applies to testing the words, dreams, visions, and encounters of prophets, but if you are going to prophesy it also applies to testing the spirit of what you are seeing or hearing, to make sure it is actually God and not a counterfeit spirit.

To be sure, it's not always practical to sit and judge prophecy for days or weeks before releasing it. For example, in times of spontaneous prayer you can't sit and pray and study to gain confidence that you are accurate in the spirit. Many times, personal prophecy erupts suddenly and must be released in the moment or the opportunity will be lost. However, before you engage in this type of spontaneous prophetic ministry you should have an established track record for success.

Yes, there is grace to miss it, but by judging your own prophecy with the help of the Holy Spirit you can miss it privately rather than missing it publicly—and to ask Him to show you where you went wrong. In other words, wouldn't you rather have the Holy Spirit show you privately how you missed it rather than bringing harm to someone or discrediting yourself publicly?

When I was young in the prophetic, I searched out Scriptures that were in line with my prophetic words and asked the Holy Spirit to give me confirmation before releasing the revelation publicly. As a matter of fact, with bold and significant national prophecies, I often still do. It's wisdom.

If you are in the bounds of edification, exhortation and comfort, there is no great harm to anyone if you miss it. But this issue of judging your own prophecy becomes critical to your prophetic reputation if and when you start naming dates, prophesying into world events, and otherwise releasing significant words. Get into the practice of judging your own prophetic revelations now. It's good training for your prophetic future.

You can learn more about judging prophetic revelation in my book, *Did the Spirit of God Say That?: 27 Ways to Judge Prophecy.*

PROTOCOL 3
DO LET OTHERS JUDGE WEIGHTY WORDS

In 1 Corinthians 14:29, Paul the apostle wrote these Spirit-inspired words: "Let two or three prophets speak, and let the others judge." Oh, that we would follow this protocol!

The word "judge" in this verse comes from the Greek Word "diakrino." According to *The KJV New Testament Greek Lexicon*, it means, "to separate, make a distinction, discriminate, to try, decide, to determine, give judgment, and decide a dispute."

Other translations of 1 Corinthians 14:29 say, "the others should weigh carefully what is said" (NIV); "let other evaluate what is said" (NLT); "let the others discern" (Berean Literal Bible); "Everyone else should decide whether what each person said is right or wrong" (GOD'S WORD Translation); "let the others pass judgment" (New American Standard 1977); "while the rest pay attention and weigh and discern what is said" (AMPC).

Benson Commentary says, "Let the prophets speak—In succession; two or three—And not more, at one meeting; and let the others judge—And compare one doctrine with another for the further improvement of all. Or, the sense may be, Let the others, who have the gift of discerning spirits, discern whether they have spoken by inspiration or by private suggestion."

And *Gill's Exposition of the Entire Bible* sheds this light on the matter: "Let the other judge: the other prophets that sit and hear, and all such as have a spirit of discerning, whether what the prophets say comes from their own spirits, or from a lying spirit, from the spirit of antichrist, or whether from the Spirit of God."

This is a serious issue and a serious command with serious words.

Who are these "others" of whom Paul speaks? These "others" are other prophets. While you can ask your pastor or wise elders to judge your prophecy, prophets ideally need other prophets to judge their significant prophetic utterances. That's because prophets don't just walk in an anointing, they stand in an office. It's a higher ranking in the spirit and a different level of hearing. But even a true prophet can miss it.

What do I mean by significant prophecies? Prophets are more likely to receive weightier words, dreams, visions or encounters that could influence or even frighten people. Therefore, the best ones to judge those words are other prophets who may be hearing the same thing or who can add wise insights that help them communicate God's heart in a way the greatest number of people will receive it.

PROTOCOL 4
DO KNOW WHEN TO HOLD YOUR TONGUE

Just because the Lord shows you something does not mean you are supposed to release it. The Holy Spirit who spoke to you is the same Holy Spirit who will give you an unction to release the prophecy. Unction essentially means anointing. If you are sensitive enough to hear the voice of the Holy Spirit, you should also be sensitive enough to discern a prophetic anointing to release it. Remember, the anointing is not for you, but to serve others.

1 Peter 1:21 tells us, "For prophecy never came by the will of man, but holy men of God spoke as they were moved by the Holy Spirit." Hold your tongue if the Holy Spirit is not moving you to speak. He can speak to your heart and not move you to open your mouth. *The Passion Translation* puts the verse this way: "No true prophecy comes from human initiative but is

inspired by the moving of the Holy Spirit upon those who spoke the message that came from God."

Merriam-Webster's dictionary offers additional insight on the word unction. One definition is, "a religious or spiritual fervor or the expression of such fervor." You may feel a bubbling up, as it has been described so many times in the prophetic movement. Jeremiah the prophet gives good verbiage to how it feels when the word of the Lord comes to you with an unction to release it:

"His word was in my heart like a burning fire shut up in my bones; I was weary of holding it back, and I could not" (Jeremiah 20:9). The New Living Translation says, "His word burns in my heart like a fire. It's like a fire in my bones! I am worn out trying to hold it in! I can't do it!"

Hearing does not equal unction. Seeing does not equal unction. Dreaming does not equal unction. An unction is a bubbling up in your spirit—not a bubbling up in your soul. Maturing in the prophetic means differentiating where the bubbling up is coming from.

PROTOCOL 5
DON'T COMPARE YOUR FLOW TO ANOTHER'S

Don't compare your prophetic flow with anyone else's. God moves differently through different people and you don't need to prophesy like anyone else—nor should you try to. God has given you a unique voice, a unique style, and a unique message. You have a unique prophetic expression.

You may not see angels, but you may have epic dreams. You may not prophesy over nations, but your personal prophecy can encourages many. You may not interpret dreams, but you may see revelation in the spirit and understand how to apply it to benefit the Body of Christ. Be willing to go deeper, but be comfortable with how God moves through you while you hunger for more in a healthy way.

2 Corinthians 10:12 reminds, "For we dare not count or compare ourselves with those who commend themselves. They who measure themselves by one another and compare themselves with one another are not wise."

Catch that. It's not wise to compare yourself with anyone else in any area, but particularly with spiritual gifts. If you compare yourself to someone else you may either be puffed up with pride and think more highly of yourself than you ought or feel less than, not good enough, and think more lowly of yourself than you ought. Both are toxic to your prophetic flow.

If we are going to compare ourselves with anyone in the prophetic, it should be Jesus. He is the prototype prophet. We will never live up to His accuracy, wisdom and grace, but we can safely look at Him as a model.

Remember, you can get into a lot of trouble—and error—trying to be something prophetically that you are not. Be confident in who you are while God keeps making you into a better you.

PROTOCOL 6
DON'T PROPHESY TO STRANGERS ALONE

Do not prophesy to people you do not know alone without a strong unction from the Lord. This is for your protection. If you prophesy to someone one-on-one, what you share can be misconstrued, taken out of context, or completely twisted. In other words, the one to whom you are prophesying could walk away telling people you said things you didn't say— and damage your prophetic credibility. I've seen this happen time and again.

David once wrote, "All day they twist my words" (Psalm 56:5). This can happen in prophetic ministry, even public meetings. That's because people sometimes hear what they want to hear instead of what was prophesied. But at least when you prophesy with a witness there's a witness!

You may have heard the phrase "parking lot prophets." These are prophets that wait until you get out in the parking lot, alone, to prophesy to you. They don't want anyone to know they are prophesying so they do so secretly. Parking lot prophets carry a bad name in the prophetic movement because there is no accountability, often plenty of error and sometimes full-blown Jezebelic manipulation.

If the Lord is pressing you to prophesy to a stranger alone, record it on your phone and save it. Let the person know you're recording it and saving it and offer to send them a copy. They may still go around telling people you prophesied something different than what you said, but at least you have proof of what was prophesied.

PROTOCOL 7
DO SHARE THE PROPHECY IN THE RIGHT SETTING

There's a place to prophesy. Beyond the "parking lot prophets" warning, not every setting is appropriate to release every prophetic revelation. Where one might prophesy certain words in certain settings, other prophecies would be inappropriate to release in those same settings.

Let me give you a practical example. Some prophecies should be released in private, with discretion. If the Lord shows you someone's spouse is cheating on them and the marriage will go through rocky times for six months before being restored, that is not an appropriate word to release in a public setting. This could cause embarrassment and shame when the Lord is trying to bring hope and faith to walk through a trial.

Much the same, prophesying certain directional prophetic words, dreams or visions publicly can put pressure on a person to respond positively with agreement even if they don't believe the prophetic revelation is true— or negatively with disagreement that challenges your word even if it is true. You don't want to put people—or yourself—in these awkward positions.

Think about it like this. You may speak one way to your family at home but the tone has to change in the workplace. It wouldn't be appropriate to call your coworkers pet names you use for your kids or your spouse. It's appropriate to scream at a football game but it would be inappropriate to scream in an opera. Your prophetic behavior and release must be appropriate for the setting in which you find yourself.

PROTOCOL 8
DO SHARE THE REVELATION IN THE RIGHT TIMING

You may have heard it said, "Timing is everything." That can be especially true in prophetic ministry. A right word released at the wrong time may not be received at all, or may be rejected fervently. Ecclesiastes says there's a time for every matter under heaven (see Ecclesiastes 3:1). Guess what? That includes prophecy.

If you've ever had to give bad news to someone, you know the importance of timing. If you can help it, you don't want to give bad news to someone who is already having a bad day. That's because their perspective is clouded and it may send them into a tailspin. Guys, you want to ask your girl to marry you at the right time, when she is receptive and not distracted and upset with her mother or employer.

In the prophetic, sometimes you have to be patient and wait for the right time to deliver a prophetic revelation; a time when a person seems ready to receive it. Timing can be both a science and an art. Ask the Holy Spirit about the timing to release important prophecies, dreams, visions and encounters.

Proverbs 15:23 says, "A word spoken in due season, how good it is!" (Proverb 15:23) That could be reversed to say, "A word spoken out of season, how bad it is!" You can release a good word at a bad time and have terrible results. The dream or vision, likewise, must wait for the appointed time of release.

Other translations of Proverbs 15:23 drive this point home: "how good is a timely word" (NIV); "it is wonderful to say the right thing at the right time" (NLT); "how delightful is a timely word" (Berean Study Bible); and "a well-timed word is a good thing" (ISV)." Proverbs 25:11 says, "A word fitly spoken is like apples of gold in settings of silver." Ask God to give you good timing. He's the Creator and Master of time. He knows when someone's heart is ready to receive a prophetic word.

PROTOCOL 9
DO SHARE THE REVELATION IN THE RIGHT MEDIUM

It's critical to share the word in the right medium. What is a medium? *Merriam-Webster*'s dictionary defines medium in this context as "a channel or system of communication, information or entertainment; a mode of artistic expression or communication."

Some prophecies, dreams and visions, can be shared over the telephone, for example. You may even be able to text some prophetic words or use an application like Voxer to share what the Lord is saying. However, for heavier or more meaningful prophetic revelation—that which goes beyond edification, exhortation and comfort—face to face is usually the best medium. In a digital age, we sometimes forget the power of face-to-face ministry.

Also, different mediums imply different audiences. If you share a prophetic word in your local church it usually only goes about that far. If you share a prophetic word on TV, radio or online magazines, it has the potential to go much further and may land on the ears of people for whom it was not intended—or who do not have the necessary context or background to discern what to do with what they have heard.

For prophets with a public ministry, prophetic words can be released from the platform, via YouTube or through social media like Facebook. However, not every word is appropriate for social media release.

Here's a tip: If you can't properly unpack a prophetic word, it should not be released to the masses on social media because it could unintentionally them astray. For example, a short Facebook post about a dream or vision that offers no practical understanding, application or prayer points can do more harm than good—even if the prophetic revelation is absolutely true.

PROTOCOL 10
DO SHARE REVELATION WITH THE RIGHT PERSON

Beyond the truth in the last protocol about prophesying over various mediums and seeing your prophecy land on someone's ears for whom it was not intended, it's also vital you don't share a personal prophetic word about someone with other people. Let me put it to you this way: Don't share prophecies about some else with someone else.

Many times, doing so amounts to prophetic gossip—or worse. I had this happen to me. A prophetic elder shared a dream he had about me with a younger prophetic person instead of me. That younger prophetic person skewed the elder prophet's dream to the point that it became a death pronouncement over my life and released a spirit of fear against me.

Proverbs 3:21 admonishes us to keep sound wisdom and discretion. One with good discretion is discreet, which means "having or showing discernment or good judgment in conduct and especially in speech: prudent," according to *Merriam-Webster's* dictionary.

Agabus did not share his Acts 21 prophecy to Paul about his arrest with 10 other people. He took it straight to Paul. Sharing personal prophetic words about someone with others for whom they are not intended is bad prophetic form. It can cause all sorts of trouble. God didn't give you that prophetic word, dream or vision about someone to share with other people first. He gave it to you to share with a specific person or a specific group of people.

With all that said, there are valid reasons to share prophetic revelation about others with outsiders. The Lord may lead you to share it for the purpose of having a significant, directional or otherwise heavy prophetic revelation judged before you release it. The Lord may also lead you to get counsel on whether to share it, how to share it, or how to pray through it. It's the motive and intention that matters.

PROTOCOL 11
DO SHARE THE WORD AND NOTHING BUT THE WORD

When the bailiff swears you in as a witness in courtroom, they ask, "Do you swear to tell the truth, the whole truth, and nothing but the truth, so help you God." How much more should we represent the truth rightly as prophets, seers and prophetic people. We have to be careful to share the word and nothing but the word, not adding to or taking away from what we hear or saw in the spirit.

Keep this in mind: When it comes to hearing the word or seeing a vision, many times you miss the true meaning through your personal interpretation. Unless the Lord specifically gives you the meaning of a parabolic prophecy or a vision, don't insert your own reasoning into the interpretation process. You could water down the faith of the one receiving the prophetic utterance.

For example, if you see an orange in the spirit over someone's head and you don't hear the Lord's commentary on the visual, don't start prophesying out of what the color orange represents or some other interpretation that has a personal meaning to you.

Saying you see an orange over that person's head may mean something lifechanging to the one to whom you are ministering. If so, that's all they need to hear. If you start trying to interpret what you've seen or heard and you get the interpretation wrong, they may miss their blessing. I've seen people get excited about the revelation until the heard an interpretation different from what they knew in their heart. Instead of being comforted, their hopes were dashed.

Don't feel pressure to interpret what you see or hear. Even if it doesn't make sense to someone immediately, many times the Holy Spirit will show them what He meant later. What's more, the revelation may have to do with their future and will serve as confirmation at a later time. Say what you heard or what you saw and leave the rest to the Holy Spirit. Once you release the word, you have done your part. The Holy Spirit is faithful to do His part.

Remember what Joseph said to the baker and the butler, who each had dreams in prison: "Do not interpretations belong to God?" (Genesis 40:8). This principle not only applies to dreams but also to prophetic words and visions, and any other type of prophetic encounter that has to be interpreted.

PROTOCOL 12
DON'T BE A PERFORMING PROPHET

Prophets don't perform. Prophets should prophesy. Performance can hinder your prophetic flow. Yes, some prophets may have a delivery style that is loud or bold or more theatrical than others by nature. That's not what we're talking about here. If you are being yourself and you are typically loud or bold or theatrical, you are not performing.

Think about the nature of performing. A performer puts on an act or a show. They are playing a role. It is not who they are. It's not authentic. The prophetic is not about performance. It's not about hyping up a crowd. It's about moving the hearts of men with the voice of God.

Our prophecy and our delivery should seek to draw attention to Jesus, not ourselves. Maybe you've heard the term showboat. *Merriam-Webster*'s dictionary defines showboat as "to behave in a conspicuous or ostentatious manner: show off." This is what we want to avoid.

For example, some people get the mic to prophesy a short word and start preaching a whole sermon. Some people shake a fake or a stutter to sound more spiritual. Some people feign tears at dramatic times in their prophetic word. Ultimately, this comes of insecurity or pride, or what was modeled to them. Don't put on a prophetic show. Show off the glory of God.

PROTOCOL 13
DON'T FEEL OBLIGATED TO ELIZABETHAN ENGLISH

In the early days of the prophetic movement, especially among the Word of Faith movement, people prophesied in Elizabethan English. You could also call it King James Version English. King James English uses a lot of thees and thous. For example, God saveth thou and thy salvation is secureth.

Part of the reason for the thees and thous and hast nots is because most Christians were reading the King James Version of the Bible until recent years. So the Word went in sounding Elizabethan and came out sounding Elizabethan.

However, some prophetic people have taken on the mindset that you have to prophesy in Elizabethan English, which sounds kind of like a Shakespeare play. There's no need to speak Elizabethan English. God will speak to you in a manner that's relatable to you—or to the one to whom you are prophesying.

That's why you'll even hear some prophets use slang or language that's unique to their culture. God is speaking to them in a language they understand.

PROTOCOL 14
DO BE AWARE OF FACIAL EXPRESSIONS

In a prophetic ministry team setting, be aware of your facial expressions and gestures. Although many people close their eyes while you are prophesying to them, some don't. Your prophesy may be saying one thing but your face may be saying something entirely different.

Of course, you can't completely control your countenance while you prophesy. But if you are on a prophetic team you can at least be more conscious of your countenance while someone else on the team is prophesying.

The Bible says a backbiting tongue brings forth an angry countenance (see Proverbs 25:23) but a joyful heart makes a cheerful face (see Proverbs 15:13). Wisdom causes the face to beam (see Ecclesiastes 8:1). In other words, your face talks.

If you are smirking while someone else on the team is delivering a prophetic word because you don't bear witness to the utterance, you could be grieving the Holy Spirit and stealing the faith of the one receiving what may be legitimate prophetic ministry. God sees your countenance. Even if it's not a good word, professionalism dictates not wearing a look of shock or a sourpuss.

By the same token, in a team setting it's courteous to the Holy Spirit to pay attention to the process of ministry even when you are not prophesying. That means you shouldn't be looking at your phone or your watch, but praying in the spirit or at least agreeing in your heart with the one prophesying. And while I understand being tired, try to hold back the repetitive yawns.

Remember, these and similar actions are unprofessional and can hurt someone's ability to receive. Isaiah 3:9 demonstrates how your countenance can "bear witness against you." We don't want to quench or grieve the Holy Spirit. We want to edify, comfort and exhort.

PROTOCOL 15
DON'T ARGUE ABOUT YOUR PROPHECY

Never argue about your prophetic word. If someone doesn't bear witness to what you have prophesied, don't try to convince, cajole, defend or otherwise persuade someone to buy into a prophecy you released, even if you absolutely know 100% it is the word of the Lord.

Here's why: If you argue your case for the accuracy of the prophetic word, dream or vision, the person is more likely to put up their guard. That makes it's more difficult for the Holy Spirit to break down those walls and confirm accurate prophetic revelation later.

The Bible speaks against arguing several on several occasions. 2 Timothy 2:4 says, "A servant of the Lord must not quarrel but be gentle to all, able to teach, patient..." Proverbs 15:1 says, "A soft answer turns away wrath, but a harsh word stirs up anger." And 1 Timothy 2:33-34 admonishes:

"But avoid foolish and ignorant disputes, knowing that they generate strife. And a servant of the Lord must not quarrel but be gentle to all, able to teach, patient, in humility correcting those who are in opposition, if God perhaps will grant them repentance, so that they may know the truth..."

Your job is done when you deliver the prophetic revelation, other than praying as the Holy Spirit leads. You are not the convincer. Nobody respects a defensive prophet.

PROTOCOL 16
DO REMAIN CALM IF SOMEONE REACTS BADLY

In the case of a strongly bad reaction from someone to whom you are prophesying, remain calm and peaceable. I've never had this happen, but it could happen, especially if you stray beyond the bounds of 1 Corinthians 4:3.

There may also be backlash later, with people telling all their friends about the bad prophetic word they received from you. Don't answer back or defend yourself. Every word of God proves true (see Proverbs 30:5, ESV).

Of course, it's possible you completely missed it and caused offense. Or it's possible that your prophetic word, although meant to be encouraging, tapped into some sort of memory or wound the Lord is trying to heal, catching the person off guard. If you are moving in the Spirit to prophesy, you must be sure to display the fruit of the Spirit if you get a bad reaction. Galatians 5:22-23 (TPT) tells us:

"But the fruit produced by the Holy Spirit within you is divine love in all its varied expressions: joy that overflows, peace that subdues, patience that endures, kindness in action, a life full of virtue, faith that prevails, gentleness of heart, and strength of spirit. Never set the law above these qualities, for they are meant to be limitless."

Protocol 17
Do Admit if You Miss It

In the Old Testament, if a prophet uttered a prophecy that didn't turn out to be true, he was deemed a false prophet. Not so in the New

Testament. (Aren't you glad?!) The New Testament gift of prophecy—and even the New Testament prophet—has a different purpose than their Old Testament counterparts. Thank God we don't have to worry about getting stoned if we miss it!

The point is the prophecy is fallible. Even the most mature Christians who are rooted and grounded in the love of Christ and the Word of God can and do offer prophetic utterances that are less than 100 percent accurate.

If it were impossible for one truly gifted by the Holy Spirit to offer an inaccurate prophesy, Paul and John would not have exhorted us to judge it. I share some of the reasons why prophets miss it in my book, *Discerning Prophetic Witchcraft.*

If you miss it, admit it. People will actually trust your prophetic voice more if you are willing to acknowledge your mistake. Humility is one of the fruits of the Spirit, but pride goes before destruction (see Proverbs 16:18). If you want God to use you in the prophetic, being willing to acknowledge your error is vital. Remember, God opposes the proud but gives grace to the humble (see James 4:6).

PROTOCOL 18
DO LEARN FROM YOUR PROPHETIC MISSES

If you obviously missed it—if it was absolutely wrong—take the opportunity to learn from your mistake. Many times, we learn more by our mistakes than we do from our successes. We do not aim to make mistakes in the prophetic realms but no one is perfect.

If you know you've made a mistake, ask the Holy Spirit exactly how you missed it. Was it a personal bias? Were you moved by the expression—or lack of expression—on someone's face? Did you get part of it right but the wrong part was so off that the person rejected the entire prophetic word? Were you listening to some other spirit? Was it your imagination instead of a true vision?

Again, if you need to repent, repent. People will respect you more for acknowledging you missed it than for trying to defend a word that is clearly wrong. Don't let missing it discourage you to the degree that you stop prophesying. When you learned to ride a bike, chances are you fell down once or twice. Get back on the bike! The righteous man falls down seven times but gets back up again (see Proverbs 24:16).

PROTOCOL 19
DO STAY ACCOUNTABLE

Accountability seems to be a dirty word in a few prophetic camps—but most welcome the concept. Think of accountability as your friend. Accountability is your safety net. Don't avoid accountability. You don't want to be a Lone Ranger in the prophetic. And, if you think about it, even the Lone Ranger had Tonto to set him straight sometimes.

First of all, we are accountable to God. Romans 14:12 says: "So then each of us shall give account of himself to God." We should also be accountable to others on our prophetic team. Proverbs 27:1 assures us "As iron sharpens iron, so a man sharpens the countenance of his friend."

Finally, we must be accountable to our apostles, pastors and elders. Hebrews 13:17 says, "Obey those who rule over you, and be submissive, for they watch out for your souls, as those who must give account. Let them do so with joy and not with grief, for that would be unprofitable for you."

Stay accountable and teachable. Receive correction so you can develop your prophetic gifting. Think of it this way: Accountability also protects you from false accusations. If you aren't accountable to anyone, who will stand for you when you are being attacked for accurately exercising your prophetic gift?

PROTOCOL 20
DO BE DIPLOMATIC

Deliver prophetic words with diplomacy. How you deliver a word can make a difference in whether or not someone receives it. What is diplomacy, you ask? *Merriam-Webster*'s dictionary defines it as skill in handling affairs without arousing hostility.

Being a diplomatic prophet means you are "exactly reproducing the original" and "employing tact and conciliation especially in situations of stress." Tact is "a keen sense of what to do or say in order to maintain good relations with others or avoid offense."

Now, sometimes a prophetic word will offend people. There's no escaping that reality. But sometimes it's offensive or hurtful because of the way, or where you prophesied it. As ambassadors of God, we have to be good diplomats for the Kingdom of Heaven.

If you have to deliver a corrective word, for example, it should be released only after much prayer and even grieving or weeping. Delivering words of warning must also be done with diplomacy to avoid perceptions of judgment on a person, as if they are in some way to blame, etc.

Diplomacy in the prophetic begins with the way we listen to God. In order to express God's heart in a matter, we need to hear His heart and not just His voice. If we miss God's heart, we can miscommunicate His will and lead people astray or cause them to shut their ears to a true prophetic revelation.

When we listen well, we will share responsibly. If we listen to God through the lens of our bias, we will speak with prejudice. If we listen to God through the filter of bitterness, we will speak with judgement. If we listen to God through the ears of grace and mercy, we will speak the bold truth in love.

PROTOCOL 21
DO COMMIT YOURSELF TO PROPHETIC ACCURACY

Commit yourself to prophetic accuracy. When I was in journalism school, my professor had a saying, "If you don't have accuracy, you don't have anything." He was referring to accuracy in news reporting. As journalists, we had to report the truth. One misquote could change an entire story and damage the source's reputation—and ultimately ours.

How much more should we commit ourselves to accuracy in the things of the spirit? We have to report the truth of God's prophetic word, vision or dream. One misquote could change the entire prophetic revelation, or the way in which one receives the entire prophetic word.

Proverbs 30:5 tells us: "Every word of God is pure." The New Living Translation says, "Every word of God proves true." If it's not God's prophetic word, it's not accurate. When we commit ourselves to accuracy, we won't prophesy flippantly.

Acts 18:25 speaks of accuracy: "This man had been instructed in the way of the Lord; and being fervent in spirit, he spoke and taught accurately the things of the Lord..." Study the Word to show yourself approved, and you will find yourself more accurate as a result.

PROTOCOL 22
DON'T LET PEOPLE PRESSURE YOU TO PROPHESY

Once someone sees you prophesy accurately, you may find people will pressure you to prophesy at meetings or even in private. I have had that happen time and time again. Don't give in to this pressure. Resist the pressure to prophesy like you'd resist the devil.

Pressure is a burden of physical or mental stress. That's according to *Merriam-Webster*'s dictionary. It can be disturbing when people always expect you to prophesy on demand, even at the dinner table or while you are driving away in your car after ministering all day.

People should not be putting a demand on you to prophesy according to their will. If God is not speaking, you don't have anything to say. Sometimes God is not speaking anything new to someone because they didn't do the last thing He instructed them to do in a previous prophetic word. Selah.

Taking on pressure to prophesy because people expect you to have a word can lead you into compromise or error. If you strain and stress to prophesy you could tap into a familiar spirit or divination. Don't worry about what could happen to your reputation if you don't prophesy. Be more concerned about what could happen to your reputation if you succumb to pressure and speak something the Holy Spirit is not saying.

PROTOCOL 23
DON'T OVERTHINK PROPHETIC REVELATION

While you should judge your prophetic revelation before releasing an utterance, be careful not to fall into the prophetic trap called overthinking. Your head can talk you right out of releasing what the Holy Spirit spoke to your heart or revealed to your spiritual eyes. In other words, you can talk yourself right out of sharing a valid prophetic word, dream or vision.

Judge the accuracy of your prophetic revelation by the spirit, not by your soul. This is part of being led by the Spirit and demonstrates a level of maturity in the prophetic. There may be times when you prophesy words, see visions or dream dreams that seem contrary to what you know, think or believe about someone.

Why is that? It may be because you are holding that person to who they used to be or because you know of current situations in their life that seems to make the prophetic word unlikely to come to pass. You could also be judging by an outward appearance.

Remember, God looks at everyone through the eyes of love. You are prophesying His will and their potential, not necessarily their current reality or condition. God will work to encourage people to lay aside weights and sin that are holding them back from their prophetic destiny. The prophetic word you release could actually be part of the process that spurs them to come up higher.

Again, don't overthink it. This is called analysis paralysis and will hinder both your prophetic flow and delivery. Analysis paralysis is based in your soul, not in your spirit. God has given you a mind to reason, but many times you can't reason out a prophetic word. It may seem strange or wrong or too fantastic to your soul, but God's thoughts are higher than our thoughts (see Isaiah 55:8-9). Prophecy taps into His higher thoughts.

PROTOCOL 24
DON'T VIOLATE SCRIPTURE

The Word and the Spirit agree (see 1 John 5:8). Let me say that one more time for emphasis. The Word and the Spirit agree. Since that's true, a prophetic word will not violate the written Word. To violate means to "break, disregard, or profane," according to *Merriam-Webster*'s dictionary. *Webster's Revised Unabridged Dictionary* defines violate as "to abuse." We want to be careful not to propagate prophetic abuses in the name of the Lord.

If your prophetic word breaks the boundaries of Scripture, you are committing a spiritual violation. Likewise, if your prophetic utterances disregard what the Bible has already said, you are in violation. Remember, prophets are called to teach God's people how to separate the holy from the profane and distinguish between the clean and unclean (see Ezekiel 44:23).

Let's be a little more specific so there's no room for misunderstanding. You violate the spirit of Scripture by prophesying something that disagrees with the Word of God. This is another reason you need to judge your prophetic utterance before uttering them. It's vital for prophets and prophetic people to know the Word of God to reduce our risk of violating it.

Although prophecy is not on par with Scripture, we must treat it as holy if it came from the mouth of God. Media's secular prophets violate Scripture with their predictions, prophets must hold a higher standard—the standard of the Word of God.

PROTOCOL 25
DON'T PRACTICE AMBIGUOUS PROPHECY

Don't practice ambiguity in the prophetic. In fact, work to avoid ambiguity at all turns. When we're ambiguous, it means we're speaking something that is "capable of being understood in two or more possible senses or ways," according to *Merriam-Webster*'s dictionary. It's true that sometimes prophecies can have more than one level of meaning, just like the Word of God itself, but it will not be confusing.

Put another way, don't offer prophetic words that are mystical, super spiritual and so ambiguous it leaves someone confused. God is not the author of confusion (see 1 Corinthians 14:33). The Holy Spirit may speak in parables, but He can speak expressly (see 1 Timothy 4:1). Personal prophecy that intends to edify, comfort and exhort needs to be plain, not cloaked in mysterious language that leaves the person with several potential interpretations.

We want people to walk away edified, not exasperated; exhorted, not irritated; comforted, not confused. An ambiguous prophetic word is one that is obscure or indistinguishable. It's inexplicable.

Most true prophecy is not ambiguous— though it may be parabolic. But remember, when Jesus spoke in Parables, He intended for His disciples to understand. Jesus told them, "It has been given to you to know the mysteries of the kingdom of heaven, but to them it has not been given" (Matthew 13:11).

PROTOCOL 26
DON'T HOLD BACK WHAT YOU DON'T UNDERSTAND

When you hear a prophetic word, dream a dream or see a vision that you don't immediately understand, don't keep silent just because it doesn't immediately make sense to you. Speak it out and let the person weight it up. Remember, even one small word you don't understand could mean something life-changing to the person to whom you are ministering.

During ministry in Sweden, the Lord showed me a popsicle in the spirit. The popsicle was hanging up in the air. When I walked the other direction, the popsicle was still there. I didn't want to call it out. It seemed foolish to me, but when I released it a woman in the audience started screaming hysterically. We came to find out her husband, who had not yet come into the meeting, was asking God to confirm whether he should open a popsicle business. What seemed foolish to me was a confirmation for someone else. Go figure.

If you are somewhat timid or unsure about what you've seen or heard in the spirit, you can use some prophetic wisdom in your delivery to cut your risk while you're gaining confidence.

For example, instead of declaring something as gospel truth, ask questions such as "Does the word _____ mean anything to you?" or "Is anyone in your family named _____?" In this way, if they say no you can mere say, "I must have been mistaken" and move on.

PROTOCOL 27
DO PRACTICE PROPHETIC DIVERSITY

Remember, God speaks in many ways. Some of the most common are "the word of the Lord coming unto you saying," rhema words from Scripture, seeing "pictures," visions, impressions or an inner witness and burdens. Words of wisdom often come through physical sensations. (You can learn more about seer vocabulary in my book, *The Seer's Dictionary*.)

Don't get so reliant on one way God speaks that you miss other ways He is communicating with you prophetically. As prophetic people, we need to train our spiritual senses. Commit yourself to stretching into various prophetic communication modes so you receive the message God wants to give you.

Hebrews 5:14 speaks of exercising our spiritual senses: "But solid food belongs to those who are of full age, that is, those who by reason of use have their senses exercised to discern both good and evil." *The Passion Translation* drives this home:

"But solid food is for the mature, whose spiritual senses perceive heavenly matters. And they have been adequately trained by what they've experienced to emerge with understanding of the difference between what is truly excellent and what is evil and harmful."

Commit to regular exercise. You can exercise your seer gift in my book *Seer Activations* or take the Seer Activation Challenge at *www.schoolofthespirit.tv*. You can also check out the School of the Seers.

PROTOCOL 28
DON'T CONTRADICT YOUR PROPHETIC TEAMMATES

Don't prophesy the exact opposite of what someone else on a prophetic ministry team has just prophesied. Put another way, don't prophetically assert or imply the opposite of the prophetic revelation someone else on your team just shared. This brings confusion to the one receiving prophetic ministry. If they are unable to judge, they could walk away conflicted at the contradiction.

God is not the author of confusion (see 1 Corinthians 14:33) and God does not contradict Himself. So when clear, undeniable contradictions are prophesied in a public setting it's clear someone is prophesying wrong. If someone prophesies something that is in error, there is a way to deal with that but it's not through contradiction.

What's more, purposely prophesying the opposite of what someone else just released can appear as prophetic competition or strife. 2 Timothy 2:23 tells us to avoid foolish and ignorant disputes because they generate strife. James 4:1 tells us pride promotes strife and James 3:16 tells us where envying and strife is there is confusion and every evil work.

You may be trying to redeem a prophecy, but if you give the appearance of evil you are violating Scripture (see 1 Thessalonians 5:22). You can deal with an error in your prophetic team, but it's best to do by redeeming the missed prophecy rather than pressing to prophesy the opposite.

PROTOCOL 29
DO REDEEM MISSED PROPHECIES

If a younger prophetic minister on a team misses the mark and you know it, try to redeem the word without embarrassing the minister. Our first priority is to create a safe environment for people. We do not want them to take a wrong prophecy and apply it to their life.

As mentioned in Protocol 28, however, we do not want to merely prophesy the opposite. This makes it sound to the person receiving the prophesy that God is double-minded or that there is prophetic strife. So how do you deal with this in diplomacy?

Here's a suggestion: When someone clearly misses it, redeem the Word by explaining at the end of the session that prophecy is fallible and that if they did not bear witness to something that they should disregard it or, as we say in prophetic circles, "put it on the shelf."

When you know someone missed it, ask them if they have any questions. In extreme cases where the prophecy may lead someone in wrong direction, you can asked the minister who missed it to leave and explain and apologize to the person who received the wrong prophecy—then prophecy a redeeming word. If everyone sticks within the bounds of edification, exhortation and comfort even a wrong word should not be harmful.

PROTOCOL 30
DON'T EMBARRASS OR SHAME PEOPLE

Never release a prophetic word, dream or vision publicly that will embarrass someone. If you receive prophetic revelation about someone who might embarrass them, declare the opposite as God's will over their lives. For example, if you see they are in sexual sin, declare God's love for them and His work to purify them. Never openly share someone's secret sin in the name of prophecy.

Shame is not part of the gift of prophecy, and has no place in personal prophetic ministry. People already know their sin, they don't need you to prophesy it. They are already ashamed if they are in sin, they don't need you to expose it.

God doesn't shame us. Just as there is no condemnation in Christ (see Romans 8:1), there is no shame in Christ. The Holy Spirit may prophesy a word that convicts someone's heart, but you usually won't be aware of what you are prophesying in those instances. But, again, God doesn't shame us.

If the Lord is pressing you to share a prophetic word that could cast aspersions on someone, you can do it privately. Please make sure it is the Lord. I point again to the example of Nathan rebuking David for his sin with Bathsheba and the murder of her husband in 2 Samuel 12. Nathan was led of the Lord, but allowed David to avoid public shame.

PROTOCOL 31
DON'T MOVE BEYOND YOUR PROPHETIC ANOINTING

Don't move beyond your prophetic anointing. For example, if you are not a five-fold prophet, do not give someone a highly directional word in a personal prophecy setting. Stick with the edification, exhortation and comfort.

The Passion Translation offers 1 Corinthians 14:3 this way: "But when someone prophesies, he speaks to encourage people, to build them up, and to bring them comfort." The anointing on a believer to prophesy works within these bounds.

The prophet's anointing extends to include weightier words for individuals, churches, regions and nations, including directional words and, at times, even words of rebuke. If you are not a seasoned prophet, you should avoid offering highly directional words that could take someone's life off course. You are responsible to the Lord for your utterance.

Yes, God's grace is sufficient for every believer to move in the simple gift of prophesy, but trespassing into a five-fold office for which you are not anointed to serve can cause trouble. The anointing is to serve others. The grace is for you to operate in an anointing, but there is no grace to operate in an anointing God did not give you.

Of course, God can anoint any believer to prophesy beyond the 1 Corinthians 14:3 bounds but you should not presume to go there without a strong unction.

PROTOCOL 32
DON'T PROPHESY HIGHLY DIRECTIONAL WORDS OVER LEADERSHIP PUBLICLY

Prophets can prophesy beyond edification, exhortation and comfort. Prophets can prophesy directional words. We see this in the pages of the Bible, with prophets directing kings with the prophetic word of the Lord and interpreting dreams. However, this is often done privately.

Without a high degree of relational trust, it's often wiser to deliver highly directional words behind closed doors. Before prophesying highly directional words to church members publicly, ask the church leadership to judge it first.

It could be the directional word is something that would edify the congregation or help them honor the leader or catch the Lord's vision for the church at a deeper level. But it could also be that the directional word goes against everything the leader has been saying in that season.

Of course, the Lord can direct you to release a highly directional prophetic word to leadership without any filter. But use wisdom. Your prophetic utterance could bring spiritual warfare or scrutiny upon the leader, even if it is correct. Remember, just because you are hearing the word of the Lord come unto you saying doesn't mean you need to open your mouth wide and release it at that time.

PROTOCOL 33
DON'T PROPHESY DIRECTIONAL WORDS OVER OTHER PASTOR'S SHEEP

Take great care and caution in prophesying highly directional words over other people's sheep (the members of another pastor's church). You could be making it harder for a sincere pastor to deal with a wounded person who wants to run ahead of God or a rebellious disciple who is not ready for promotion.

Keep Hebrews 13:17 in mind: "Obey those who rule over you, and be submissive, for they watch out for your souls, as those who must give account. Let them do so with joy and not with grief, for that would be unprofitable for you."

In a conference culture, I've seen many prophets prophesy highly directional words over attendees with no regard for the outcome. Because they don't pastor a church, some prophets neglect to consider the pastor who has to pick up the pieces of a broken heart or a life mess based on a wrong prophetic word or even a good prophetic word applied at the wrong time.

Indeed, I have also heard horror stories from church leaders about itinerant prophets prophesying to their members in a prayer line to "move to California in three days" or "quit their job and start a business in 90 days." In most cases, it is out of order to prophesy highly directional life changing words to someone else's flock without consulting with them first.

God can always make an exception, but an exception is not a protocol.

PROTOCOL 34
DO TAKE CAUTION WITH PROPHETIC REBUKES

Do not correct or rebuke people with a prophetic word in a public setting without a strong unction from the Lord. Public rebukes do happen, but this is rare and seems to occur only after someone has rejected the Lord's direct counsel and the private counsel of those around him—repeatedly.

Remember when Nathan rebuked David over the adultery with Bathsheba and the murder of her husband Uriah? The rebuke was not offered in a mean spirit or in public, nor was Nathan happy about delivering the message. Yes, the Lord can move through a prophet to issue a strong prophetic rebuke but this is not the norm. Yes, the Lord disciplines those He loves but the spirit of the prophet must be right and the vessel pure and mature to move at this level.

I'll always remember when a visiting pastor came into a church I attended many years ago and declared he was going to prophesy over everyone in the meeting. Most of his prophetic words were critical and judgmental, indicting and condemning people with rebukes. He was not a prophet, was moving beyond his anointing, and took pleasure in setting everyone straight. He later lost what influence he has in Europe and was found in a scandal. Use wisdom.

PROTOCOL 35
DO BE CAUTIOUS ABOUT PROPHESYING MATES

I'll keep saying this: The simple gift of prophecy works in the bounds of edification, exhortation and comfort. Edification, exhortation and comfort does not include directing the personal life affairs of people. You can ruin someone's life with a word about who they should marry. If you are a prophet, God may use you in this realm but typically not without relationship and not often in public settings.

More than once, I've watched as others prophesied "a husband is soon coming" to women whose actual husband was standing next to them! These prophetic words may be coming from the prophet's loneliness or their perception that you are not whole without a mate, or just presumption. I've also seen people prophesy specific people should marry and seen it end in disaster.

That said, it's not always a disaster. I have also witnessed prophets prophesy to recently devastated women about God preparing a husband for them in the future. The word encouraged them. That technically still falls within the 1 Corinthians 14 bounds. God can use the prophet in this area, but the prophet should proceed with caution and the prophetic believer should stay away from this type of utterance.

Generally speaking, do not prophesy mates. Prophesying spouses wrongly and spurring two people to marry outside the will of God can be devastating in more ways than one. It can ruin lives. If people don't know who God is leading them to marry, they should wait until they hear from the Lord.

PROTOCOL 36
DON'T PROPHESY ABOUT BABIES TOO QUICKLY

Yes, we do see prophets in the Bible prophesy about pregnancies. Prophets, after all, prophesied the birth of Jesus. And Elisha prophesied to Shunamite woman: "About this time next year you shall embrace a son" (2 Kings 4:16). The Shunamite woman in fact bore a son according to the prophetic utterance of Elijah.

Yes, I have known modern-day prophets who have prophesied babies to barren women and those women bore children according to the prophetic utterance of the prophet. I myself have prophesied babies and the sex and names of babies and been accurate.

However, this is not a prophetic flow to be entered into lightly and, unfortunately, I have seen as many misses as hits in the realm of prophesying babies from the mouths of prophetic believers moving beyond their anointing.

I have seen prophets prophesy babies to women who were desperate for a child and left them even more hopeless after they remained childless. If you are going to prophesy a baby, you better make sure you have heard from the Lord.

PROTOCOL 37
DON'T PROPHESY OFFICES LIGHTLY

Jesus gave (and still gives) five-fold ministers—apostles, prophets, evangelists, pastors and teachers—to the church according to Ephesians 4:11. Making a bold, public prophetic declaration that someone is a five-fold minister can cause difficult issues to arise on several levels.

First, you have no idea the spiritual standing of the person you are prophesying to. They may be walking in defiance to their pastor and your prophetic word could cause trouble for their shepherd. Even if the word is accurate, that "office" prophecy could also unleash spiritual warfare on someone they are in no way ready to handle. Whether the "office" prophecy is right or wrong, if the person embraces the mantle there will be warfare. What's more, the prophecy of an office could also puff them in up in pride.

You may see the office someone carries, but that does not give you a license to share it publicly. You need to be sure it's the will of the Lord to share the prophetic intelligence in the moment, or if you should rather prophesy something more general about the strong future and call God has on the person's life. You may want to check with the person's leader to see if they are ready to receive this word and pay the price required to walk in the calling.

God does make exceptions. I've seen generals in the prophetic call out younger ones as prophets publicly. Those generals may have been the only ones who recognized the call by the Spirit of God and the subject of the prophecy needed the affirmation. But you should not make a habit of this. It must be God-inspired or it could cause trouble for all.

PROTOCOL 38
DON'T PROPHESY DATES LOOSELY

Unless the Holy Spirit is very clear, do not give specific timeframes as to when a prophetic word may come to pass. Much of prophecy is conditional and depends on someone doing their part before God does His part to bring the prophecy to pass.

The rule of thumb is this: If God gives you a specific time line, such as "in seven days it shall be" or "before the end of the year" and spurs you to share the date as part of the prophecy, then by all means share the date. It could be the date drives a sense of needed urgency for the ones hearing the word to take some necessary action. However, many emerging prophets have made the mistake of adding a time frame the Lord never spoke.

This is dangerous for two reasons. First, the person you are prophesying to may throw the entire prophecy out the window if it doesn't come to pass in the time frame you prophesied. If you prophesied the time frame out of presumption or error, you are doing the person a disservice because they will give up on the prophetic word, abandon the will of the Lord, and potentially miss an opportunity because of an expiration date.

Second, if you are in the habit of prophesying dates and consistently miss it, it could bring your entire prophetic ministry under reproach. Keep this in mind, many times the date or time you give doesn't add much to the prophesy and it's not necessary to include it. At other times, the number of days, the time of year or some other time specification is vital to someone taking urgent action. Discern whether the time is vital before releasing a specific time or date.

PROTOCOL 39
DO BE CONFIDENT WITH YOUR PROPHETIC RELEASE

People new to the prophetic can be nervous about releasing prophecy. That's natural and normal. I call it prophetic stage fright. However, if you are going to prophesy publicly you need to work up confidence before you release broader utterances to larger crowds in order to be taken seriously.

For example, don't deliver the prophetic word with a wishy-washy tone as if you are not sure you believe actually believe it. For example, don't say things like, "Well, I am not sure but I think I might have heard the Lord say..." That's OK in a home group or a private setting while you are learning but will not instill confidence in those you are prophesying to. In fact, it will do just the opposite.

If you are not confident the Lord is speaking, don't release an utterance in His name. Judge your own word before you open your mouth. We prophesy according to the proportion of our faith (see Romans 12:6). If you don't have the faith to release the prophetic word with confidence, wait until you do so that those who hear your utterance hear a word wrapped in faith. (Again, if you are just learning it's OK that you are not as confident.)

Protocol 40
Don't Overemphasize Angels

Speaking of angels, Hebrews 1:14 tells us, "Are they not all ministering spirits sent forth to minister for those who will inherit salvation?" We should not ignore the ministry of angels. Angels ministered to Jesus on two occasions in Scripture: in the wilderness and in the Garden of Gethsemane.

Although God may lead you to prophesy about angelic assistance for someone, we must be careful not to overemphasize angels at the expense of magnifying these ministering spirits above our Lord Jesus Christ.

Angelic beings are messengers, and can independently deliver prophetic messages to you or to people under the leadership of Jesus. But our prophetic ministry must be centered in Christ, not angels. Consider these two passages featuring John in the Book of Revelation:

"I fell at [*the angel's*] feet to worship him. But he said to me, 'See that you not do that. I am your fellow servant, and of your brothers who hold the testimony of Jesus. Worship God! For the testimony of Jesus is the spirit of prophecy'" (Revelation 19:10, emphasis mine).

"I, John, am he who saw and heard these things. When I heard and saw them, I fell down

71

to worship at the feet of the angel who showed me these things. But he said to me, 'See that you not do that. For I am your fellow servant, and of your brothers the prophets, and of those who keep the words of this book. Worship God!'" (Revelation 22:9).

Again, we value the ministry of angels and even the God-sent message of angels, but Christ must be exalted in our prophetic ministry.

PROTOCOL 41
DO POINT PEOPLE TO JESUS

If we are operating in the Holy Spirit, our prophetic ministry will point people to Jesus. Christ Himself offered these words in John 16:12-14 (AMPC):

"I have still many things to say to you, but you are not able to bear them or to take them upon you or to grasp them now.

"But when He, the Spirit of Truth (the Truth-giving Spirit) comes, He will guide you into all the Truth (the whole, full Truth). For He will not speak His own message [on His own authority]; but He will tell whatever He hears [from the Father; He will give the message that has been given to Him], and He will announce and declare to you the things that are to come [that will happen in the future].

"He will honor and glorify Me, because He will take of (receive, draw upon) what is Mine and will reveal (declare, disclose, transmit) it to you."

Like the Holy Spirit, prophets are not speaking on their own authority. The Holy Spirit is transmitting the message to the prophet's spirit on behalf of Jesus. We are just the mouthpiece. As such, our prophetic ministry must honor and glorify Jesus.

PROTOCOL 42
DO KNOW YOUR PROPHETIC BOUNDARIES

If you are a member of a church, understand the prophetic beliefs, culture, boundaries, and protocols of that church before presuming to operate in prophetic ministry there. If you want to operate legally in the spirit, you need to respect the authority of the house in which you find yourself in.

The same goes for the house prophets. You may be a recognized prophet in the house in which you serve, but each church is unique and may have some variance in the way they prefer for prophets to release prophetic utterances. For example, do you need to submit it to a prophetic leader first or do can you prophesy at the end of worship freely?

When you are visiting another church as a guest speaker, ask the host if they have prophetic protocols and if you have permission to prophesy. We do not want to quench the Spirit, but the Bible does say we should do all things decently and in order (see 1 Corinthians 14:39-40). It can be a fine line, but we have to learn to walk it in prophetic honor.

PROTOCOL 43
DON'T PROPHESY WITHOUT PERMISSION

Beyond churches, there are roundtables, conferences and prayer events in which prophecy may come forth. Just because you are at the meeting does not give you an open door to prophesy.

Put another way, do not prophesy without permission. What do I mean by permission? If the meeting is not yours, you do not have the authority to prophesy without the permission of the person who is holding the meeting. Let me give you an example:

I've been in meetings with zealous prophets don't follow this protocol. They are given the mic for a moment to pray and they take over the meeting with prophecy after prophecy after prophecy while the time runs out on the reason why people actually gathered. This is out of order and makes the prophet look reckless and irresponsible. 1 Corinthians 14:40 tells us to do all things decently and in order.

Some will claim they had fire shut up in their bones and could not help it. But the rule of decency and order must prevail. Just eight verses before the "decency and in order" instruction Paul, inspired by the Holy Spirit, also said this: "The spirits of the prophets are subject to the prophets" (1 Corinthians 14:32).

The Message says it like this: "Take your turn, no one person taking over. Then each speaker gets a chance to say something special from God, and you all learn from each other." And *The Passion Translation* puts it in plain English: "Keep in mind that the anointing to prophesy doesn't mean that the speaker is out of control—he can wait his turn."

We must submit to the authority of the meeting. If we are not given permission to prophesy, then we don't prophesy. If the meeting leader misses it or is being disobedient to God, that is between God and that leader. If it's not your meeting, you should not usurp the authority of the leader. If God wants your prophetic message released, He will make a way—even if it's not the way you think. Remember, God's ways are higher than our ways (see Isaiah 55:9). Trust Him and stay decent and in order and you will gain respect.

PROTOCOL 44
DO ASK BEFORE TOUCHING PEOPLE

Do not touch the person you are prophesying over without asking permission. Some people do not like to be touched for a variety of reasons. Touching them could cause them to get upset or to be unable to receive the prophetic word. It may just make them uncomfortable.

If they give you permission to touch them, touch their head or shoulders only. Females should not touch the belly of a male and males should not touch the belly of a woman. If your prophecy requires a prayer wherein you would need to lay hands on the mid-section of man, find a male altar worker and ask them to put their hand on the receiver's belly, then you put your hand on top of their hand. Same goes with men ministering to women.

In 1 Timothy 5:22, Paul taught Timothy, "Do not lay hands on anyone hastily..." While this is in the context of ordination, it can also be fitting in any type of ministry.

PROTOCOL 45
DON'T WORK TO INTERPRET YOUR UTTERANCE

Sometimes when we prophesy or see a vision while praying for someone we do not know what it means. It's not that it's ambiguous, it just may not have a clear meaning to us. This will set you free: It doesn't have to. Remember, God is not prophesying to you, He's prophesying through you. You don't necessarily have to understand what it means to release it.

Many sincere, accurate prophets miss it trying to explain what they think a prophetic word means or what a vision or dream means. Explaining is not prophesying. While there is a time to counsel someone on a prophetic word you offered that doesn't make immediate sense to them, your first course of action is to prophesy and let the word sink in with the person for whom its intended.

Remember this: Sometimes what you prophesy or see doesn't mean anything to you but it means everything to them. Sometimes they don't immediately know what it means either but if you leave it alone and give them time with the Lord to ponder, He will make it clear to them.

This is a general rule of thumb: If you have clear interpretation from the Lord, it's fine to share it. If you aren't rock solid on what it means, leave that to the person to pray through. You could dampen or invalidate a powerful prophetic word with a wrong interpretation as they may know it means one thing but you are telling them it means something else.

PROTOCOL 46
DO TAP INTO TEAM SYNERGIES

Synergy is a beautiful thing in prophetic ministry. Where there's synergy, the whole is greater than the sum of its parts. We understand this concept as it relates to spiritual warfare, as one can put a thousand to flight and two can put ten thousand to flight (see Deuteronomy 32:20). There is also a prophetic synergy when the team is yielded to the Holy Spirit.

You'll discover in prophetic team ministry often times the Holy Spirit will build one word up on another's. In other words, one person may pick up and add a part to what the last person prophesied. Go with the flow. Tap into those team synergies.

In the Bible, prophets ran in companies (see 1 Samuel 19:20; 1 Kings 20:35; 2 Kings 2:3; 2 Kings 2:16; 2 Kings 4:38). We know in part and we prophesy in part (see 1 Corinthians 13:9). Often, if you prophesy your part someone else on the team will have another part to help fill in the full picture.

PROTOCOL 47
DO NOT CHARGE FOR PROPHECY

You've probably heard of a "holy handshake." If not, here's my definition of a holy handshake: someone approaches you and shake your hand with money in their palm as a secret donation to bless you. It's their discreet way of sowing into your ministry. There is nothing wrong with someone giving you a "holy handshake." There is everything wrong with selling prophecy.

Selling prophecy or setting up Internet pages with "suggested donation" amounts on your website is not faith. If you can't walk by faith for provision, how are you prophesying by faith? (The Bible says we prophesy according to the proportion of our faith [Romans 12:6]). You are sending mixed signals to people and damaging your credibility when you put out a shingle and propose to prophesy for money.

If the motive of your prophetic ministry is money, you've missed the mark and you are bringing a reproach on Christ's name. The motive of prophetic ministry, like any other ministry, is love. 1 Corinthians 13:2 tells us, "And though I have the gift of prophecy, and understand all mysteries and all knowledge, and though I have all faith, so that I could remove mountains, but have not love, I am nothing." (Read more about this practice in my book, *Discerning Prophetic Witchcraft*).

PROTOCOL 48
DO NOT ADD OR TAKE AWAY FROM PROPHECY

Don't add to or take away from the prophetic revelation you receive, whether it's a word, a dream or a vision. You are not the author or editor of prophetic revelation.

Many years ago, I changed the word "a" to "the" in a written prophecy and the Holy Spirit convicted me. I've also had magazine editors try to edit prophetic words and have had to draw a hard line on this practice. Let God be God.

Proverbs 30:5-6 tells us, "Every word of God is pure; He is a shield to those who put their trust in Him. Do not add to His words, lest He rebuke you, and you be found a liar." That seems pretty clear, but just in case it's not read the warning in the Book of Revelation 22:18-19:

"For I testify to everyone who hears the words of the prophecy of this book: If anyone adds to these things, God will add to him the plagues that are written in this book; and if anyone takes away from the words of the book of this prophecy, God shall take away his part from the Book of Life, from the holy city, and from the things which are written in this book."

While this refers to Scripture, it applies to prophecy. If God said it, God said it. If God showed it, God showed it. Don't change it. Release the prophetic revelation the way He gave it to you, without adding your opinion or omitting parts of the revelation that you feel might offend people or cause them to reject it. God is the only author who doesn't need an editor.

All that said, God may instruct you not to reveal everything He told you or showed you. That is entirely different from changing what was said or neglecting to share vital aspects of what He revealed due to fear of man.

PROTOCOL 49
DO BE CAUTIOUS ABOUT YOUR BIASES

What is a bias? A bias is "an inclination of temperament or outlook, especially: a personal and sometimes unreasoned judgment; prejudice, bent, tendency," according to *Merriam-Webster*'s dictionary.

Going a little deeper, prejudice means "a preconceived judgment or opinion; an adverse opinion of leaning formed without just grounds or before sufficient knowledge; an irrational attitude of hostility directed against an individual, a group, a race, or other supposed characteristics."

Can you see how dangerous it is to let bias cloud your prophetic word?

You can't be cautious about something of which you aren't aware. It's vital to understand your biases. Ask the Holy Spirit to reveal those biases to you. If you are aware of this weakness, you are less likely to allow a personal bias to pollute the pure prophetic word the Lord wants to release through you.

Now, take it a step further and repent for those biases. Ask the Lord to help you see things the way He does, and to heal any wounds that would lead you to walk in a bias toward an individual, group or race. Where biases exist unchecked, you are in danger of prophetic error.

PROTOCOL 50
DON'T LET YOUR EMOTIONS GET INVOLVED

We are all emotional beings. God gave us emotions—and God Himself has emotions. But we have to be careful not to allow our own emotions—or ego or subjective experiences—supersede the Word of God in our prophetic ministry.

One very relatable example of the danger of letting your emotions seep into our prophetic ministry is bitterness. Bitter prophets abound. Maybe the church rejected them. Maybe they were wounded in a personal relationship. Regardless of the reason why, we're seeing more bitterness polluting the prophetic. It's each individual's responsibility to keep their heart clean.

You can always discern a bitter prophet by the words that come out of their mouth in the name of the Lord. The writer of Hebrews warned, "Pursue peace with all people, and holiness, without which no one will see the Lord: looking carefully lest anyone fall short of the grace of God; lest any root of bitterness springing up cause trouble, and by this many become defiled" (Hebrews 12:14-15). We want our prophetic ministry to edify, comfort, exhort, warn, direct or correct, not defile.

James 3:10-12 offers this insight that should be applied to your prophetic flow: "Out of the same mouth proceed blessing and cursing. My brethren, these things ought not to be so. Does a spring send forth fresh water and bitter from the same opening? Can a fig tree, my brethren, bear olives, or a grapevine bear figs? Thus no spring yields both salt water and fresh."

Bitterness is just one of many emotions that can pepper your prophecy to the point of toxicity. Fear, discouragement, anger and the like can muddy your prophetic flow. Negative emotions have no place in prophecy. If you are unable to manage your emotions and keep the negative soulish feelings out of your mouth, you shouldn't prophesy until you calm down or find the healing you need to operate in a right spirit.

PROTOCOL 51
DON'T SUCCUMB TO THE FEAR OF MAN

Reject the fear of man in your prophetic ministry. The fear of man will dilute and could pervert your prophetic flow. Indeed, it's hard to maintain a pure prophetic flow with the fear of man running through your veins. That's because fear is like sludge that clogs your prophetic pipes.

Proverbs 29:25 warns us, "The fear of man brings a snare, but whoever trusts in the Lord shall be safe." In Matthew 10:28, Jesus said, "Do not fear those who kill the body but cannot kill the soul. But rather fear Him who is able to destroy both soul and body in hell."

If you are afraid of what people will think, say or do in response to the word of the Lord in your mouth, then you are in danger of obeying the wrong voice and releasing the wrong words—or not releasing the right words. Like Job, the thing that you feared could come upon you (see Job 3:25) because fear opens the door to the enemy.

Protocol 52
Don't Prophesy the Party Line Only

If you are part of a denomination, network, or political party, you may be tempted or even pressured to prophesy the party line. Various denominations have beliefs that differ from others—even within the Spirit-filled community. Different apostolic-prophetic networks take different stances on doctrines or social issues. And we know how divisive politics are in the Body of Christ.

With that in mind, be cautious not to prophesy the party line only. The party line is "the policy or practice of a political party," according to *Merriam-Webster*'s dictionary. The party line can also be the policy or practice of your church, your network, or your denomination. Another definition is "the principles or policies of an individual or organization."

It can be tempting not to prophesy something you know your pastor or your spiritual father will not agree with, but we must avoid that temptation if we want to remain pure. (Of course, that doesn't mean you do it in their church or at their conference unsolicited.)

In the days of King Saul, Saul wanted Jehoshaphat go to battle with him. The King of Judah wanted to consult with the prophets. The prophets Saul called forth were all prophesying the party line. We read the account in 1 Kings 22:6-8:

"Then the king of Israel gathered [a]the prophets together, about four hundred men, and said to them, 'Shall I go against Ramoth Gilead to fight, or shall I refrain?' So they said, "Go up, for the Lord will deliver it into the hand of the king."

"And Jehoshaphat said, 'Is there not still a prophet of the Lord here, that we may inquire of Him?'

"So the king of Israel said to Jehoshaphat, 'There is still one man, Micaiah the son of Imlah, by whom we may inquire of the Lord; but I hate him, because he does not prophesy good concerning me, but evil.'"

When Saul calls forth Micaiah, the other prophets warn him to prophesy the party line. Pay careful attention to these verses in 1 Kings 22:13-14:

"Then the messenger who had gone to call Micaiah spoke to him, saying, 'Now listen, the words of the prophets with one accord encourage the king. Please, let your word be like the word of one of them, and speak encouragement.' And Micaiah said, 'As the Lord lives, whatever the Lord says to me, that I will speak.'"

Micaiah's response should be your heart posture. We cannot prophesy the party line to stay in good standing with the leader, group, network, or denomination. We must stay true to God's line at all costs. Remember, Saul asked Micaiah to prophesy.

PROTOCOL 53
DO BE OPEN TO DISCUSSING YOUR PROPHECIES

If someone wants to discuss with you a prophetic word you released, be open to doing so. While it's not possible to spend a great deal of time discussing every prophetic word you release with every person to whom you release it, there are times when you should take that extra step.

Your crystal clear, well communicated, well-timed prophecy may still land on confused ears. Taking even a moment to discuss the prophetic word with its recipient could help bring clarity that makes it possible for them to receive the word gladly and war with it according to 1 Timothy 1:18 until it manifests.

The other side of the discussion coin this: taking a moment to explain or reiterate could help you avoid misunderstandings and false accusations. I know from experience people often hear something different than what you said (or what the Lord said through you). Sometimes people hear what they want to hear. Sometimes they could not hear you clearly because the music was too loud. Sometimes they just don't comprehend what it really meant, even though they bear witness to the word.

Remember, as a prophet, seer or prophetic person you are a minister. We have to be willing, at times, to go the extra mile with someone; to take a moment to help them understand what the Lord is saying. That is especially true with any word that may be directional or correctional in nature.

PROTOCOL 54
DON'T PUBLICLY NAME MINISTERS IN PROPHECIES THAT BRING THEM INTO CONTROVERSY

Do not publicly name ministers connected to controversial prophecies, especially if the word suggests the minister is in some sort of error, sin or relational strife. Even if you are seeing and hearing accurately, God is not showing this to you so you can expose people's issues. He's showing you for the purpose of prayer.

There is no need to air dirty laundry you hear in the prayer closet—and what if you are wrong? Think of the damage you can do by suggesting relational strife or insinuating sin based on a prophetic dream, vision or a still small voice.

Remember, love covers a multitude of sins (see 1 Peter 4:8). There is a time when exposure does come in the Body of Christ, but we should not make accusations based on prophetic words, dreams and visions. Evidence must manifest in the natural.

And, again, the most likely purpose you are receiving this type of prophetic revelation about leaders in your church or in the Body of Christ at large is for the purpose of intercession rather than intervention or exposure. And what if you missed it? Consider the aspersions you could cast on reputable ministers.

PROTOCOL 55
DO COMMIT TO YIELDING TO THE SPIRIT

Commit your heart to yielding to the Spirit. If you do this, you will have a fruitful prophetic ministry. Part of yielding to the Holy Spirit is prophesying when He wants you to prophesy, and not prophesying when He's not leading you to prophesy.

Yield means "to surrender or relinquish to the physical control of another: hand over possession of; to surrender or submit (oneself) to another; to give up and cease resistance or contention," according to *Merriam-Webster*'s dictionary.

In Galatians 5:16, Paul wrote these Spirit-inspired words, "As you yield freely and fully to the dynamic life and power of the Holy Spirit, you will abandon the cravings of your self-life." Just as we have to yield our mouths to the Holy Spirit to prophesy, we sometimes have to yield to the Holy Spirit not to prophesy.

Beyond this, though, your entire life should be yielding in submission to Him. All believers, especially those who speak in the name of the Lord, should intentionally cultivate a yielded spirit. We must yield to the hand of the Potter. In my book, *The Making of a Prophet*, I wrote:

The late Kathryn Kuhlman used to sing a song at her meetings called "Spirit of the Living God." The lyrics say, "Spirit of the Living God. Fall Fresh on Me ... Melt me, mold me, fill me, use me ..." This should be the cry of the prophet.

Yield to the Spirit of God as He moves to shape your character, rooting out issues that keep the prophetic anointing from flowing freely. Resisting God never turns out well. Yielding to the hand of the Potter, no matter how He is moving in your life, may be uncomfortable but you will maintain a certain peace if you pursue an intimate relationship with Father.

PROTOCOL 56
DO RESPECT YOUR PROPHETIC ELDERS

We need to honor and respect our prophetic elders. Many of them paid a great price to pave the way for the ministry we're operating in now.

1 Peter 5:5 tells us, "Likewise you younger people, submit yourselves to your elders. Yes, all of you be submissive to one another, and be clothed with humility, for 'God resists the proud, but gives grace to the humble.'"

And 1 Timothy 5:17-18, "Let the elders who rule well be counted worthy of double honor, especially those who labor in the word and doctrine." Romans 12:10 tells us to outdo one another in showing honor.

In Romans 13:7, Paul wrote: "Render therefore to all their due: taxes to whom taxes are due, customs to whom customs, fear to whom fear, honor to whom honor." You don't have to agree with someone to honor them. You can respect their position without respecting some of their beliefs.

How do you honor your prophetic elders? You can sow into their ministries. You can share their posts on Facebook. You can speak well of them to others. You can pray for them. You can thank them for their contribution to the prophetic movement and to your life. You can follow them as they follow Christ. You can defend them in the face of accusation. You can love them.

Honor unlocks a reward. I once heard the Lord say, "Honor releases My blessing, My anointing and My great rewards. Many have sown dishonor, disrespect and discord and are seeing the fruit of unrighteousness in their life. They have not understood or recognized the glory that comes from walking in honor."

If you are going to walk in the prophetic, walk in love and walk in honor.

PROTOCOL 57
DO SEEK GOD FOR REDEMPTION AMID HARD PROPHETIC REVELATION

God is a God of redemption. After all, in Christ we have redemption through His blood, and forgiveness of our sins according to His riches in grace (see Ephesians 5:7). Over and over in the Bible, we see Scriptures pointing to the redemptive nature of God. Here are just a few to drive the truth home.

Colossians 1:14, "In whom we have redemption through His blood, the forgiveness of sins." And Titus 2:14, "Who gave Himself for us, that He might redeem us from every lawless deed and purify for Himself His own special people, zealous for good works. And But of Him you are in Christ Jesus, who became for us wisdom from 1 Corinthians 1:30. "God—and righteousness and sanctification and redemption."

God is not just a God of redemption under the New Covenant. He has always been a God of redemption. The Old Testament Scriptures prove it. Psalm 111:9 tells us: "He has sent redemption to His people; He has commanded His covenant forever: Holy and awesome *is* His name." And Psalm 107:2 says, "Let the redeemed of the Lord say *so,* Whom He has redeemed from the hand of the enemy."

What does it mean to redeem? The Greek word for redeem is lutroo. According to *The KJV New Testament Greek Lexicon*, it means to release on receipt of ransom, to redeem, liberate by payment of ransom, to liberate, to cause to be released to one's self by payment of a ransom, to redeem, and to deliver: from evils of every kind, internal and external. God is good. He is a redemptive God.

With this in mind, when you receive a hard word, such as a rebuke or a judgment, press in for the redemption. As prophets, we want to tell the truth, but God's truth is redemptive. God takes no pleasure in bringing disaster. God is not just looking for a man to release a judgment, He's looking for a man to release intercession.

Ezekiel 22:30 reveals God's heart: "So I sought for a man among them who would make a wall, and stand in the gap before Me on behalf of the land, that I should not destroy it; but I found no one."

If we prophesy without any redemption aspect—without a call to repentance or prayer points to equip people to avert disaster—we could breed hopelessness or even recklessness. If God gives you a strong prophetic revelation, ask the God who gave you that word, dream or vision to give you His heart and show you how to pray so you can release it with God's redemptive spirit.

PROTOCOL 58
DO CONSIDER CULTURAL NUANCES WHEN PROPHESYING TO PEOPLE GROUPS

Cultural nuances do not change the prophetic revelation, but they may change the way you deliver the prophetic revelation. People in different cultures receive truth differently. Some cultures—or some church cultures, even in America—are still relatively new to prophetic ministry. Therefore, you need to use wisdom when prophesying in these instances.

A nuance is a subtle distinction or variation, according to *Merriam-Webster*'s dictionary. Cultures around the world—or even in different denominations in your own nation—may be slightly different. Again, without considering cultural nuances you could accidentally offend someone or cause them not to receive the prophetic revelation in the way the Lord intended.

On the Day of Pentecost, when the Holy Spirit was poured out in the Upper Room, one of the results was that everyone heard their own languages being spoke (see Acts 2:6). And Paul once said, "And to the Jews I became as a Jew, that I might win Jews; to those who are under the law, as under the law, that I might win those who are under the law" (1 Corinthians 9:20).

In the context of prophetic ministry, it's often not as much about what you say—again, you can't change the word of the Lord—but about when you say it or how you say it. In some cultures, being overly boisterous could be offensive. In other cultures, being boisterous is expected from the preacher. In some cultures, what you wear will cause the crowd to receive you or not to receive you.

Take some time to study the culture of a country or understand the culture of a church in which you are ministering. You want people to receive your prophetic ministry, so if you have to make slight adjustments to deliver the prophetic revelation of the Lord you will be prepared to do so.

PROTOCOL 59
DO OBEY THE LORD TO DELIVER CHALLENGING PROPHETIC REVELATION

Obedience to God is important, and sometimes it's uncomfortable to obey God to deliver a challenging or risky prophetic word. I've done this more than once.

We must obey the Lord. Jesus said if you love Him you will keep His commandments (John 14:15). That's pretty heavy. Luke 6:46, "But why do you call Me 'Lord, Lord,' and not do the things which I say? That's pretty heavy. Here's the heaviest one of all in Matthew 7:21-23:

"Not everyone who says to Me, 'Lord, Lord,' shall enter the kingdom of heaven, but he who does the will of My Father in heaven. Many will say to Me in that day, 'Lord, Lord, have we not prophesied in Your name, cast out demons in Your name, and done many wonders in Your name?' And then I will declare to them, 'I never knew you; depart from Me, you who practice lawlessness!'"

I'm not suggesting you are going to go to hell if you refuse to prophesy a risky word. God's grace is wide. He understands the issues holding you back, such as fear of persecution or fear of missing it. However, if you want God to use you at the highest levels, obedience in every area, including delivering risky words, is critical.

In my book, *Becoming a Next-Level Prophet*, I write: "Obedience is better than sacrifice (see 1 Samuel 15:22). Indeed, obedience is the prophet's prerequisite. Your obedience builds the Lord's trust in you. God will often give His prophets small—or even strange—instructions. Step by step, obeying God's voice will transition you from low-level assignments to next level missions. Disobeying God's voice could land you in the belly of a whale. (You remember Jonah, right?)"

PROTOCOL 60
DO CULTIVATE A FEAR OF THE LORD

Prophets need to cultivate a healthy fear of the Lord. The fear of the Lord is not always a popular topic, but it's vital–especially in the hour in which we live. The Bible, and especially the Proverbs, have plenty to say about the fear of the Lord and the benefits of embracing it.

The fear of the Lord is to hate evil (see Proverbs 8:13). The fear of the Lord is the beginning of wisdom (see Proverbs 9:10). The fear of the Lord is the beginning of knowledge (see Proverbs 1:7). The secret of the Lord is with those who fear Him (see Psalm 25:14).

The Hebrew word for fear in the context of the fear of the Lord throughout Proverbs is *yare*. One definition of the Hebrew word yare means "to fear, to respect, to reverence." The Greek word phobos can be translated "reverential fear." *Vine's Complete Expository Dictionary* defines it as "not a mere 'fear' of His power and righteous retribution, but a wholesome dread of displeasing Him." That's intense!

Cultivate a healthy fear of the Lord. There is no want for them who fear Him (see Psalm

34:9). In the fear of the Lord, there is strong confidence and a fountain of life (see Proverbs 14:26-27). By the fear of the Lord are riches, honor and life (see Proverbs 22:4).

I could go on and on about Scriptures that talk about the benefits of cultivating the fear of the Lord in your heart. This is vital for all believers, but how much more for those who speak in His name?

PROTOCOL 61
DON'T STEP OUT TOO SOON

Don't step out into prophetic ministry in a major capacity without a commissioning or without a blessing from your pastor or leader. Remember, there is a space of time between the calling and the commissioning. If you step out ahead of God's timing, you may experience situations and/or spiritual warfare that you are not equipped to handle.

Work with your spiritual father or mother or your leader to get prepared for what God wants to launch you into. That doesn't mean you can't exercise your gift. It means your leaders may recommend some boundaries in exercising your gift until you gain wisdom that comes only through experience.

For example, your leader may deem it appropriate for you to minister in prophecy rooms, but determine you are not ready to minister on the platform on Sundays. Or, your leader may determine you are ready to prophesy in the house but advise you against ministering at conferences outside the church.

God may have called you to the office of the prophet before He formed you in your mother's womb—and you may indeed be a prophet to the nations—but there is a making process. If you get ahead of God's timing, you could do yourself or others unintentional harm.

PROTOCOL 62
DO REMAIN HUMBLE IN THE FACE OF RECOGNIZED ACCURATE PROPHETIC REVELATION

Entire books have been penned on humility and if you are a prophet you should keep a few of them in your library and read through them periodically. Andrew Murray's classic *Humility* should be on every prophet's shelf. Another good one is R.T. Kendall's *The Power of Humility*. It's vital that prophet guard their hearts from pride because pride perverts and pollutes the prophetic voice.

The Bible has plenty to say about humility. James 4:6 tells us, "But He gives more grace.

Therefore He says: 'God resists the proud, but gives grace to the humble." And Proverbs 11:2 tells us, "When pride comes, then comes shame; but with the humble *is* wisdom."

If you want to walk in grace and wisdom, walk in humility. You may be the most accurate prophet in your church or network, but the moment you lose your humility is the moment you may find yourself in a dark night of the soul or, worse, on the edge of spiritual pride.

In Luke 14:11 Jesus said, "For whoever exalts himself will be humbled, and he who humbles himself will be exalted."

God has a unique way of humbling prophets who get out of line and don't remember to give the glory to God. If we're supposed to give glory to God for eating and drinking (see 1 Corinthians 10:31), how much more should we give Him the glory in prophetic ministry? We're just a vessel. He's the revelator.

PROTOCOL 63
DO CHRONICLE YOUR PROPHETIC REVELATION

Chronicle your prophetic utterances. This is biblical. In fact, good portions of the Bible are chronicles of prophetic words, dreams and visions. Keep a journal of your prophetic words, dreams and visions, especially if they are significant or profound in nature.

Old Testament prophets understood the importance of chronicling their prophetic revelations. In fact, they took prophetic revelation so seriously often more than one copy was made. Once, Jeremiah was once seized and his prophetic words burned. The Lord did not take too kindly to it.

"Now after the king had burned the scroll with the words which Baruch had written at the instruction of Jeremiah, the word of the Lord came to Jeremiah, saying: 'Take yet another scroll, and write on it all the former words that were in the first scroll which Jehoiakim the king of Judah has burned.

"And you shall say to Jehoiakim king of Judah, 'Thus says the Lord: 'You have burned this scroll, saying, 'Why have you written in it that the king of Babylon will certainly come and destroy this land, and cause man and beast to cease from here?'"

We also know when Moses broke the Ten Commandments, God wrote them out again. If God revealed it through word, dream, vision or encounter, it's worth chronicling.

PROTOCOL 64
DO RELY ON MINSTRELS TO HELP CREATE A PROPHETIC ATMOSPHERE

At times, you need a minstrel—or a worship team—to charge a prophetic atmosphere. Worship tends to help everyone, even you, focus on the Lord. Elisha appreciated the minstrels. When the king wanted the prophet to prophesy, he asked for a musician. 2 Kings 3:14-19 gives the account:

"And Elisha said, 'As the Lord of hosts lives, before whom I stand, surely were it not that I regard the presence of Jehoshaphat king of Judah, I would not look at you, nor see you. But now bring me a musician.'

"Then it happened, when the musician played, that the hand of the Lord came upon him. And he said, "Thus says the Lord: 'Make this valley full of ditches.' For thus says the Lord: 'You shall not see wind, nor shall you see rain; yet that valley shall be filled with water, so that you, your cattle, and your animals may drink.' And this is a simple matter in the sight of the Lord; He will also deliver the Moabites into your hand. Also you shall attack every fortified city and every choice city, and shall cut down every good tree, and stop up every spring of water, and ruin every good piece of land with stones."

Learn how to work with the house musicians. Talk to them and tell them the types of sounds that help you flow, or how to play behind you while you're prophesying. The right music can enhance the delivery of a prophetic word. The wrong music can actually work against you.

PROTOCOL 65
DO ASK THE LORD FOR CONFIRMATION BEFORE RELEASING RISKY REVELATION

If you get a prophetic word that's especially risky, one that could scare people or damage your reputation in the prophetic, it's wise to get confirmation before releasing it.

Confirmation is the process of finding assurance that what you heard or saw was accurate, and not just your imagination. Seasoned prophets typically don't need to seek confirmation on everyday prophecies. However, on some issues of critical importance I have seen leaders in the prophetic movement make a call for confirmation.

I received a prophecy about the 2016 election on the very morning of the election. It didn't seem likely to be true from a natural mindset, but I knew what I heard. Still, I asked the Lord for confirmation before releasing it. In fact, I also sent it to three prophetic elders to judge.

PROTOCOL 66
DON'T QUENCH THE HOLY SPIRIT OF GOD

1 Thessalonians 5:19 says not to quench the spirit. *The Passion Translation* puts it this way, "Never restrain or put out the fire of the Holy Spirit." Then New Living Translation says, "Do not stifle the Holy Spirit."

Are you getting the picture? Let's drive this home. The Berean Study Bible says, "Do not extinguish the Spirit." The Contemporary English Version says, "Don't turn away God's Spirit." And The Message says, "Don't suppress the Spirit, and don't stifle those who have a word from the Master."

If the Holy Spirit is urging you to release a prophetic word, don't muzzle Him. Don't throw water on the fire. Don't blow out the embers. Jeremiah said the word of the Lord was like fire in his bones. Listen to the intensity of his words: "The words are fire in my belly, a burning in my bones. I'm worn out trying to hold it in. I can't do it any longer!" (Jeremiah 20:9).

That said, this does not give you permission to prophesy out of order. Remember, Paul said all things must be done decently and in order (see 1 Corinthians 14:40). But we must give the Holy Spirit leadership. He is speaking for Jesus the Prophet through us. Who are we to stifle Him, or turn away from the unction?

Of course, this is easy to do when you have a prophetic revelation everyone will accept. In Jeremiah's case, he didn't have a popular prophecy but he had to release it anyway. It truly was burning within him. Out of sheer obedience, the young prophet would not quench the Spirit of God moving on Him.

PROTOCOL 67
DO CONDUCT RESEARCH TO HELP PRESENT YOUR PROPHETIC REVELATION

When possible, before you release a significant prophecy that could cause a stir, it's wise to give your audience some context. Context means "the interrelated conditions in which something exists or occurs," according to *Merriam-Webster*'s dictionary. It also means, "the parts of a discourse that surround a word of passage and can throw light on its meaning."

You've heard it said we should never take a verse of Scripture out of context. In the same way, some prophetic revelation almost demands context if we expect people to understand how to apply the truth the Holy Spirit is sharing through us.

If you are prophesying about a war between two nations, for example, it can be helpful for your hearers to understand the history of the relations between these nations. It can also be helpful in putting together prayer points.

When you are presenting a significant prophetic word, especially one that demands prayer, conducting some research about the particulars of what the Lord is saying— including Bible study to demonstrate God's heart over such matters or to develop a prayer strategy that's Word-based—is important.

PROTOCOL 68
DO EXPOUND ON THE PROPHETIC REVELATION WITH APPLICATION PRINCIPLES WHEN POSSIBLE

Many prophets deliver prophetic words. Fewer teach principles that help believers apply significant corporate prophetic words. If you are leading a church and receive a significant prophecy for the Body, consider taking the time to unpack the prophetic revelation. Teach people what to do with what you released so that it bears abundant fruit.

I find many people get excited when they hear a prophetic word, or when you share a profound dream or vision—but then they don't know where to go from there. Often, they forget all about it and never see the word come to pass. When they do remember the prophecy, they think the prophet missed it or they are disappointed or frustrated.

Sometimes, you have to teach people to war with a prophetic word, according to 1 Timothy 1:18: "This charge I commit to you, son Timothy, according to the prophecies previously made concerning you, that by them you may wage the good warfare." I write more about this in my book, *Waging Prophetic Warfare*.

Teaching the principles of applying a prophetic word can help people see the prophecies come to pass, and encourage them not to give up hope if the devil is resisting God's will.

PROTOCOL 69
DO BE WILLING TO RECEIVE PROPHETIC MINISTRY FROM OTHER PEOPLE

Even prophets can benefit from prophetic ministry. You might be your own best prophet, but don't take on the attitude that God tells you personally everything you need to hear. Sometimes, He really does speak to people—even prophets—through other people.

What's more, be willing to receive prophetic revelation from someone not as experienced as you. If God can prophesy through a donkey, and Scripture demonstrates that He can, then God can prophesy to you through a novice in the prophetic. While the messenger matters, you could miss the message if you get hung up on the messenger.

Prophets may make strategic, accurate prophetic announcements over your life that you never saw coming. Or prophets may prophecy confirmation to you. If Paul the apostle received prophetic ministry—and he did through the prophet Agabus—why wouldn't you? It's healthy for you to receive from others, especially when you're pouring out all the time.

PROTOCOL 70
DO USE VARIOUS MEDIA TO DISTRIBUTE VITAL PROPHETIC REVELATION

We live in an Internet era—a new media age. With the admitted dangers of social media among emerging prophetic voices who carry great zeal but may lack wisdom in what to share or when to share it, it's critical we discern when to use various forms of media as a vehicle to get a prophetic revelation to the masses.

This is especially true when a prophetic revelation carries a warning or a legitimately urgent call to prayer. When a prophetic message is pressing, it's vital for as many people as possible to hear the prophet's cry. In the Old Testament, they blew trumpets and sounded alarms at critical junctures. Consider The Message translation of Jeremiah 4:5-7:

"Sound the alarm in Judah, broadcast the news in Jerusalem. Say, 'Blow the ram's horn trumpet through the land!' Shout out a bullhorn bellow!—'Close ranks! Run for your lives to the shelters!' Send up a flare warning Zion: 'Not a minute to lose! Don't sit on your hands!' Disaster's descending from the north. I set it off! When it lands, it will shake the foundations. Invaders have pounced like a lion from its cover, ready to rip nations to shreds, Leaving your land in wrack and ruin, your cities in rubble, abandoned."

Not every prophetic revelation needs to be blazed abroad with urgency, but we must use media to our advantage, including blogs, e-mail lists, social media, radio, mobile apps, group messaging, so on. I believe if Jesus walked the earth today, He would use social media. In fact, God used a form of media—a book—to record His will for the ages. It's called the Bible.

PROTOCOL 71
DO PREPARE PRAYER POINTS WHEN PROPHECIES DEMAND AN INTERCESSORY RESPONSE

If you are going to issue a prophetic warning, keep in mind it may frighten people. Since that's not your goal, you have to take measures to give people hope that a warning of disaster or some other impending doom can be avoided.

Think about it this way: God is not giving you the warning just so people can hunker down and try to weather the storm. God is giving you the warning, most of the time, so you can thwart the enemy's plans, lead people into repentance, or at least minimize the impact of a demonic blow. It's God's grace to the Body to give shamar prophets warnings.

In order to empower prayer warriors rather than disempower and discourage the saints, make it a habit to study out and prepare a list of prayer points that you can issue along with the prophetic revelation. When possible, give Scripture references for your prayer points. The Word is sharper than any two-edged sword.

Some say a prophet's primary role is to release the warning and then their assignment is complete. I disagree. The prophet's role is to do everything in his or her power to bring God's will to pass in the wake of a prophetic warning, and prayer is vital. Empowering people to make intercession regarding the warning—not just releasing the warning itself—is part and parcel of the prophet's responsibility.

PROTOCOL 72
DO SEEK TO UNDERSTAND GOD'S HEART AND NOT JUST HIS WORDS

It's easy enough for a prophet to hear the words coming out of God's mouth. Understanding His heart in a matter requires a different level of hearing. It's important as a messenger to deliver the message in the spirit in which God intends it. That demands we not just recite mere words, but also let the heart of God infuse our prophecy.

First, understand this: God is love. His heart for people is a heart of love, not hate. Jesus came into the world not to condemn the world, but so that the world would be saved (see John 3:17). If His heart is not to condemn those who don't yet know Him, His heart is definitely not to condemn those who have accepted Him as Lord and Savior.

Since God is love, everything He thinks, says and does is motivated by love. That means even discipline or judgment is motivated by love. God uses the least amount of discipline to produce the greatest turning back toward His heart of love. God's heart, therefore, is for reconciliation and restoration. God is a God of hope.

When God moves on you to prophesy tough words, understanding God's heart will enable you to prophesy in love so people will actually receive the message and act in a way that pleases God. If you don't understand God's heart, you can misrepresent His Spirit even if you decree the actual words with complete accuracy.

PROTOCOL 73
DO APPLY TOUGH PROPHETIC WORDS TO YOUR OWN LIFE FIRST

Of course, not every word you prophesy will apply to you. Most won't. But when you are prophesying a tough corporate word to the Body that demands some action, such as self-examination, change in behavior, repentance of heart, etc., be sure to apply that prophecy to your own heart first.

Whether you are releasing a prophecy to your church or to the entire Body of Christ, be willing to embrace it for yourself before you step out and prophesy it to the masses. This also helps you release the word with humility.

Remember this, a prophet is not above his or her own prophetic utterance. In other words, if you are prophesying a corporate word for the

Body of Christ then it also applies to you at some level. The responsible action is to take some time—whether that's a few hours or a few days—to process the word internally and make any adjustments or take any actions you needed to take. This is a demonstration of humility.

Releasing prophetic revelation in humility results in words that are released with a discernible purity and authority. If you have submitted to the prophetic revelation, you have the right (not just the responsibility) to urge others to obey the Lord. You will also be better prepared to release the prophetic revelation in such a way that people will receive it because you are not talking to the people, you are talking with the people.

PROTOCOL 74
DO WORK TO BECOME THE MESSAGE YOU CARRY

In the Old Testament, we saw several prophets become the word, and even live it out. I call these parabolic prophets. Hosea married a prostitute at the word of the Lord, as part of a prophetic act. In another prophetic act, Ezekiel laid on one side then the other. In Ezekiel 4:1-8, we read:

"You also, son of man, take a clay tablet and lay it before you, and portray on it a city, Jerusalem. Lay siege against it, build a siege wall against it, and heap up a mound against it; set camps against it also, and place battering rams against it all around. Moreover take for yourself an iron plate, and set it as an iron wall between you and the city. Set your face against it, and it shall be besieged, and you shall lay siege against it. This will be a sign to the house of Israel.

"Lie also on your left side, and lay the iniquity of the house of Israel upon it. According to the number of the days that you lie on it, you shall bear their iniquity. For I have laid on you the years of their iniquity, according to the number of the days, three hundred and ninety days; so you shall bear the iniquity of the house of Israel. And when you have completed them, lie again on your right side; then you shall bear the iniquity of the house of Judah forty days. I have laid on you a day for each year.

"Therefore you shall set your face toward the siege of Jerusalem; your arm shall be uncovered, and you shall prophesy against it. And surely I will restrain you so that you cannot turn from one side to another till you have ended the days of your siege."

God is not likely to call you to marry a prostitute or lay on one side and then the other for days on end. The point here is that if you have a life message, if you have a key prophecy, you should live it. You should apply it to yourself. You should walk in it by the grace of God.

PROTOCOL 75
DO RESPECT OTHERS' PROTOCOLS

The churches you visit or conferences at which you minister may have different protocols from yours—and not just with regard to prophetic ministry.

When you are in someone else's house or speaking at a conference, ask your host what their protocols are, such as if there is a time limit on ministry. If your style is to you call people out of the audience and prophesy over them, make sure that's acceptable to the host. If you plan to make an altar call, ask them how that fits into their timeline.

Every church doesn't do ministry the same. You may be used to flowing a certain way and most churches may enjoy that. But if you are going somewhere for the first time, and especially if they are not accustomed to prophetic ministry or you are emerging as a speaker and don't have much experience, it's safe to ask.

You would be surprised at how many churches don't know how you flow even though they invited you. Don't take it for granted or you might not get invited back again, even if the people were blessed.

PROTOCOL 76
DO INQUIRE OF THE LORD BEFORE YOU HEAD OUT FOR PROPHETIC MINISTRY ASSIGNMENTS

Make a habit of asking the Lord what He wants to do in a meeting before you step foot onto the ministry site. This is part of your spiritual preparation.

God may not tell you anything, but He may tell you everything. He may, for example, tell you to look for the person with the red shirt. He may not tell you what to prophesy next, but He may alert you to look for that individual and then give you the word on the spot.

Many times when I am driving to Awakening House of Prayer (my church), the Holy Spirit will speak to me about someone that is coming. He will give me a word or a phrase for them, then prophecy will break forth as I am faithful to share the tidbit the Lord gave me.

Don't be discouraged if the Lord doesn't show you something before you arrive to your meeting. The fact that you asked demonstrates a responsible heart and a desire to minister to others. The Lord will be faithful to show you what you need to see or tell you what you need to hear to minister to His people at the right time.

PROTOCOL 77
DO WEEP OVER WORDS OF JUDGMENT BEFORE RELEASING THEM PUBLICLY

Some prophets are far too quick to release a word of judgment. If we take pleasure in releasing "judgement" prophecies, there is a problem in our heart. Although God is a God of judgment, He does not take delight in dropping the hammer.

Jeremiah is widely known as the weeping prophet. He's earned that moniker because his prophetic messages were full of judgment, yet he grieved over the people. Besides the Book of Jeremiah, he also wrote the Book of Lamentations. Lamentation means, "an expression of sorrow, mourning, or regret," according to *Merriam-Webster*'s dictionary.

In his weeping, Jeremiah revealed the heart of God for His people. God did not want to see His people suffer. Jeremiah felt the Lord's pain in the process. Even amid all the judgement and weeping, Jeremiah delivered a message of hope:

"Thus says the Lord: 'Refrain your voice from weeping, and your eyes from tears; For your work shall be rewarded, says the Lord, and they shall come back from the land of the enemy. There is hope in your future, says the Lord, that your children shall come back to their own border."

Prophets who carry a judgment mandate should identify with the Lord's pain and weep before releasing their message. Again, there should be no pleasure in releasing such prophecies. When John and James wanted to call fire down from heaven to judge the Samarians who would not give Jesus passage through their region, Jesus rebuked them and said, "You do not know what manner of spirit you are of" (Luke 9:55).

PROTOCOL 78
DO FOLLOW UP WITH PEOPLE TO WHOM YOU PROPHESY WHEN POSSIBLE

When possible, follow up with the people to whom you prophesy. If you are regularly prophesying highly directional words, this is especially important.

Why follow up? It's a good way to get prophetic feedback so you can evaluate your accuracy. On the other hand, if you are a spiritual mentor or pastor in their life, you may need to follow up to help them process and pray through the word.

Again, this kind of follow up and feedback isn't always possible, especially if you are prophesying over hundreds or thousands of people a year. But if you have the opportunity to follow up, do so.

Here's a simple way to get feedback. Make a general call during ministry for people to email your office and let you know if the word came to pass.

PROTOCOL 79
DO BE AWARE OF SPIRITUAL CLIMATES

It's important to be aware of spiritual climates and atmospheres and discern the way the Lord wants to move in any given ministry session. When we're aware of spiritual atmospheres, we'll shift when God shifts, speak when God speaks and see what He wants to show us so we can minister more effectively to His people.

Alternatively, when there is witchcraft in spiritual climates we have to be especially careful with prophetic ministry. Nations in which there are religious or witchcraft strongholds, idol worship and other obvious manifestations of wickedness are infested with multitudes of false gods and demon powers.

There are many voices speaking in the spirit world. In spiritual climates congested with principalities, powers, rulers of the darkness and spiritual wickedness in high places (see Ephesians 6), we must be sure we are tuned into the right voice.

Mature prophetic ministers should have no problem judging the voice of the Lord from demonic voices, but it's worth noting. I have seen inexperienced ministers tap into the voice of divination unknowingly because it sounded like something God would say or because they were overwhelmed with witchcraft against their mind. When in doubt, don't open your mouth..

PROTOCOL 80
DO RECOGNIZE YOUR PHYSICAL LIMITATIONS

We all have physical limitations. Our bodies are the temple of the Holy Spirit (see 1 Corinthians 3:16). Ministry is a marathon, not a sprint. We should recognize our own physical limitations and, in doing so, honor God with our bodies (see 1 Corinthians 3:17).

Although our spirit man doesn't get tired, our physical bodies do. It's wise not to burn yourself out in the name of the Lord. In fact, if we follow the Lord's rhythm, we will not burn out. Presenting your body as a living sacrifice does not mean running yourself into the ground. There's a balance.

Jesus understood the need to rest. In Mark 6:31-32 (TPT) we read: "There was such a swirl of activity around Jesus, with so many people coming and going, that they were unable to even eat a meal. So Jesus said to his disciples, 'Come, let's take a break and find a secluded place where you can rest a while.' They slipped away and left by sailboat for a deserted spot."

Prophets are popular in the Body of Christ because of the way their ministry blesses the church. Here's a practical tip: Be careful not to overschedule yourself. You may resist the notion but an overwhelming schedule that leaves you emotionally drained does not a healthy prophetic ministry make.

PROTOCOL 81
DO NOT ABUSE THE PROPHETIC GIFT

Prophetic ministry is rife with prophetic pitfalls and abuses. The enemy wants to pervert your prophetic voice one way or another and he sets you up for a fall at strategic points on your pathway to maturity.

Developing strong character will help you avoid the pitfalls, abuses, and even potholes, which are less damaging but can hinder your progress in the prophetic. In my experience, I've witnessed many people fall and some get back up again. If we can remove our foot from evil as fast as we recognize the temptation to step into it, we escape the polluting powers of the enemy in our prophetic ministry.

The Jezebel spirit—or just your flesh—will tempt you to use prophecy to control and manipulate people. As I said in my book, *The Making of a Prophet*, prophetic people who flow in control and manipulation are welcoming the influence of Jezebel in their lives and ministries.

"Control and manipulation are tools the enemy uses to pervert prophetic ministry," I wrote. "To control someone is to exercise restraining or directing influence over, or to have power over him. Prophets need to exercise self-control through the power of the Holy Ghost, but have no business seeking to control anyone else. If you see traces of control and manipulation in your life, go on a crusade to rid yourself of these traits because they are earmarks of the Jezebel spirit."

2 Peter 2:3 (KJV) tells us, "And through covetousness shall they with feigned words make merchandise of you: whose judgment now of a long time lingereth not, and their damnation slumbereth not." As you grow in the prophetic and start gaining attention, the temptation will come to make merchandise of people—to exploit them—by using your gift for financial

gain. This is one of the fastest ways to pervert your prophetic voice.

God is a judge, but He's not judgmental. He's not critical. He's not condemning His people. Jonah was a critical, judgmental prophet. He was angry because God gave Nineveh a space to repent—and they repented (see Jonah 4:1-2). He wanted to see them go up in smoke. Likewise, James and John had a wrong spirit when they wanted to call down fire from heaven because a Samaritan village refused to receive Jesus. Jesus rebuked them, saying, "You know not what spirit you are of" (Luke 9:55).

New Age practices have infiltrated the prophetic ministry. The Bible calls this "strange fire" (see Leviticus 10:1). The word strange in the passage means "unauthorized, foreign or profane." Prophetic operations that are not authorized by God—that are fabricated or pull from the flesh, the spirit of divination or some other source—are strange fire. Avoid strange fire like the plague. It will kill your ministry fast. I talk more about these issues in my book, *Discerning Prophetic Witchcraft*.

PROTOCOL 82
DO SEEK PROPER PROPHETIC ALIGNMENT

Some call it covering. I prefer to use the term alignment, a spiritual principle of coming along side someone to help them walk out their destiny.

Prophetic alignment is important to your progress. Prophets are unique in the Body of Christ, and no one can cover a prophet quite like another prophet. That's not to say you can't have a pastor or an apostle as your alignment, but it's usually most beneficial when the leader to whom you submit carries a strong prophetic anointing and understanding of the office in which you stand.

We find the word alignment in the New Testament 13 times in the form of the Greek word "katartizo." According to *The NAS New Testament Greek Lexicon*, it means to render, i.e. to fit, sound, complete; mend (what has been broken or rent), to repair; to complete; to fi out, equip, put in order, arrange, adjust; and ethically to strengthen, perfect, complete, and make one what he ought to be.

In the context of the "covering" discussion, Scriptures include:

Ephesians 4:11-12 reads, "And He gave some as apostles, and some as prophets, and some as evangelists, and some as pastors and teachers, for the equipping of the saints for the work of service, to the building up of the body of Christ..." The word "equipping" denotes putting someone into proper alignment.

Luke 6:40 says, "A pupil is not above his teacher; but everyone, after he has been fully trained, will be like his teacher." The key word here is "trained." And Hebrews 13:21 speaks, "Equip you in every good thing to do His will, working in us that which is pleasing in His sight, through Jesus Christ, to whom be the glory forever and ever. Amen."

Just like the proper alignment of your spine brings health benefits to your whole body, proper spiritual alignment brings benefits to your prophetic ministry. You'll have someone to watch over your soul, watch your back, teach and train you and otherwise help you if you fall.

PROTOCOL 83
DON'T BE A PEOPLE PLEASING PROPHET

Don't be an ear-tickling, people-pleasing prophet or seer. Doing so may make you popular with man, but it won't necessarily make you popular with God.

In Galatians 1:10, Paul asked a question, then basically gave an answer: "For do I now persuade men, or God? Or do I seek to please men? For if I still pleased men, I would not be a bondservant of Christ." The New Living Translation puts it this way: "Obviously, I'm not trying to win the approval of people, but of God. If pleasing people were my goal, I would not be Christ's servant."

The Passion Translation gives this Scripture a modern twist: "I'm obviously not trying to flatter you or water down my message to be popular with men, but my supreme passion is to please God. For if all I attempt to do is please people, I would not be the true servant of the Messiah." And I like The Message translation: "Do you think I speak this strongly in order to manipulate crowds? Or curry favor with God? Or get popular applause? If my goal was popularity, I wouldn't bother being Christ's slave."

Paul warned, "And whatever you do, do it heartily, as to the Lord and not to men..." (Colossians 3:23). That includes prophetic ministry. If God has entrusted you with a prophetic ministry, so keep in mind 1 Thessalonians 2:4: "But as we have been approved by God to be entrusted with the gospel, even so we speak, not as pleasing men, but God who tests our hearts."

As a prophet or prophetic person, we must never allow John 12:43 be true of us: "For they loved the praise of men more than the praise of God." People pleasing opens the door to compromise and ultimately, if the practice continues, deception.

PROTOCOL 84
DO ENGAGE IN ONGOING PROPHETIC EDUCATION

We're in the second wave of the prophetic movement, yet most Schools of the Prophets are training the gift instead of the office. Doctors, lawyers and other professionals are required to undergo continuing education programs to sharpen their skills and learn new technologies. Prophets should also engage in continuing education.

We see the concept of the School of the Prophets several times in Scripture. In 1 Samuel 19, Samuel is training prophets. 2 Kings 2 points to Elijah's School of the Prophets. And 2 Kings 4 points to Elisha's School of the Prophets.

We still need to train the gift, but part of the reset in the prophetic is a greater emphasis on training those in the office—and not just how to prophesy, but diplomacy, Christology, prophetology, character, integrity, and the like.
As you mature in your office, you will be teaching others. But that doesn't mean you don't have more to learn. A mature prophet may learn

more through the Bible than through schools, but the idea is that we should never stop learning about Jesus, our Prototype Prophet, or learning the Word of God and the ways of God. Books, webinars, intensives and schools benefit you on many levels.

PROTOCOL 85
DON'T COPY SOMEONE ELSE'S PROPHETIC WORD

I've witnessed for many years a troubling trend in the prophetic movement—a trend that is proliferating among pontificating voices who parrot true prophets. Essentially, there's a lot of plagiarism in the prophetic.

This, mind you, is hardly a new trend. Jehovah God pointed it out thousands of years ago in Jeremiah 23:30:

"'Therefore,' declares the Lord, 'I am against the prophets who steal from one another words supposedly from me'" (NIV). The New Living Translation puts it this way: "'Therefore,'" says the Lord, 'I am against these prophets who steal messages from each other and claim they are from me.'" The Holman Christian Standard Bible offers this spin: "'Therefore, take note! I am against the prophets'—the LORD's declaration—'who steal My words from each other.'"

It's been said imitation is the highest form of flattery. But to imitate someone's prophetic word as if you got it straight out of a "profound prophetic dream," a throne-room experience or a still small voice coming unto you saying isn't flattery. It's a falsehood.

While I know all too well that God speaks to many different prophetic voices about the exact same word, Scripture or theme, I am convinced prophetic plagiarists are acting like high-schoolers who didn't have time to read their literature assignment and are depending on Cliff Notes instead.

Don't be that prophet. God has given you a unique prophetic expression and a relevant message. You may have to pray it in, but He wants to work through you in the uniqueness of you.

PROTOCOL 86
DO SHARE YOUR PROPHETIC REVELATIONS WITH OTHER PROPHETS & SEERS

It's important to share your revelations and impactful prophetic words with other prophets. This is not only true in the context of having prophetic words judged, but also in the context of seeing the big picture.

1 Corinthians 13:9 clearly tells us, "For we know in part and we prophesy in part." You prophesy one part, but another prophet may prophesy another part. When you share your revelations with other prophets, you may find a more complete picture of what God is saying.

The AMPC puts it this way: "For our knowledge is fragmentary (incomplete and imperfect), and our prophecy (our teaching) is fragmentary (incomplete and imperfect)." Usually, God doesn't give any one prophet the entire truth on the matter. That doesn't make the prophecy you have inaccurate. It just means there are other dimensions of truth, perhaps prophetic strategies, that make the revelation more complete.

The Passion Translation says, "Our present knowledge and our prophecies are but partial..." And The New Living Translation adds some spice to the point: "Now our knowledge is partial and incomplete, and even the gift of prophecy reveals only part of the whole picture!" We want the whole picture.

PROTOCOL 87
DO SOFTEN RELIGIOUS LANGUAGE WHEN MINISTERING TO THE LOST

Softening language is not the same as diluting a prophetic word. By softening the language, I mean it's not necessary to be religious or overly spiritual. Many people have been burned by religion and will immediately shut down if they hear super spiritual talk or if you start shaking and quaking while talking.

There is no need to preface your prophecy with, "Thus saith the Lord." In fact, you don't even need to say, "God told me." When dealing with the lost, or people in the marketplace, you can simply tell them what you are sensing and encourage them in their situation. Everyone loves encouragement.

When dealing with the lost in prophetic evangelism, the accurate prophecy opens the door to share the gospel. In the marketplace, the accurate prophesy positions you as one who they can turn to when they need encouragement during the trials of life. Surely, the conversation will turn to God over time.

Now, I am not saying to leave God out of the mix. If you are led to share the gospel or talk about Jesus, do it. I am saying sometimes it's more effective when ministering to the lost or those in the marketplace not to preface your prophecy with religious talk. If they receive the prophecy, their heart is better prepared to receive Jesus.

PROTOCOL 88
DON'T PROPHESY ABOUT INTIMATE PERSONAL ISSUES OVER A LEADER IN A PUBLIC FORUM

Be careful not to expose a leader's sin or prophesy about intimate issues over a leader that may cause his flock to view him in a less than honorable or vulnerable light.

While it's common practice to prophesy over a leader when you minister at their church, if the Lord gives you a word that might embarrass them, undermine their authority or expose them in some way, speak to them in private.

1 Peter 4:8 tells us, "And above all things have fervent love for one another, for love will cover a multitude of sins."

It may not be a sin, it may be a hurt or wound or some personal issue in a leader's marriage. But the same principle applies. Love covers. Leaders walk though fire and trials like everyone else and do not need their congregation to know the intimate details of their life.

Put another way, you want any prophetic utterance released in front of the congregation to edify the leader. There are exceptions, of course. God could release you to share a prophetic word the leader would not like but that is a rare occasion. I will keep pointing back to 1 Samuel 12 on these issues. When Nathan rebuked David over the sin with Bathsheba and the murder of Uriah, he did it privately.

PROTOCOL 89
DON'T BRAG ABOUT HOW ACCURATE YOU ARE

There's a troubling trend among emerging prophets: bragging. When God first called me into prophetic ministry, my mentor asked my best friend: "How is she doing? Is she getting puffed up?"

There was a good reason for that concern. Paul warned in 1 Corinthians 8:1, "Knowledge puffs up." *The Passion Translation* says, "How easily we get puffed up over our opinions!" That could just as easily say, "How easily we get puffed up over our accurate prophecies."

The AMPC of this verse says, "[Mere] knowledge causes people to be puffed up (to bear themselves loftily and be proud)." The New Living Translation says, "Knowledge makes us feel important." And the New American

Standard Bible says, "Knowledge makes arrogant."

A proud prophet is a dangerous prophet. Proverbs 27:2 warns us, "Let another man praise you, and not your own mouth; a stranger, and not your own lips." And James 4:16-17 tells us, "But now you boast in your arrogance. All such boasting is evil. Therefore, to him who knows to do good and does not do it, to him it is sin."

The root of some of the prophetic bragging is insecurity, which masquerades at times as pride. And spiritual pride is perhaps the worst kind of pride. It can derail your ministry. 1 Peter 5:6 admonishes us, "Therefore humble yourselves under the mighty hand of God, that He may exalt you in due time."

There's nothing inherently wrong with a Facebook post pointing to an accurate prophecy, especially when you had previously mobilized intercessors to pray over a matter. This can be encouraging to the intercessors—and that should be your motive. When your motive is to exalt yourself, you are heading for a fall and damaging your credibility among discerning Christians.

PROTOCOL 90
DON'T PUT PROPHECY ON PAR WITH SCRIPTURE

A prophetic word is not on par with the written Word of God (Scripture). Scripture is infallible and inerrant but prophecy is not infallible and people are capable of error.

1 Corinthians 13:8 tells us prophecy will pass away but Isaiah 40:8 assures, "The grass withers, the flower fades, but the word of our God stands forever."

Therefore prophecy is not equal to Scripture. Yes, if God said it, God said it, but prophecy can be situational, conditional and personal. A single prophetic utterance does not always apply to every individual. The Word of God, on the other hand, applies to every human being ever to walk the earth.

1 Peter 1:25 tells us the word of the Lord endures forever. In the realm of prophesy, we know in part and prophesy in part (see 1 Corinthians 13:9). Scripture should have final authority in the life of a believer, not prophecy. Prophecy may be His will in a situation or a season. Scripture is God's will for every moment.

PROTOCOL 91
DON'T PROPHESY TO WIN MAN'S FAVOR

Jesus said in Matthew 6:1-2 (AMPC): "Take care not to do your good deeds publicly or before men, in order to be seen by them; otherwise you will have no reward [reserved for and awaiting you] with and from your Father Who is in heaven."

If you are prophesying to win favor with a person or a group, you are prophesying with wrong motives and are in a position to tap into divination, a false prophetic spirit.

I have seen prophets manipulate their way into conferences by prophesying flattering words to the host and getting into their heart. I have seen prophets prophesy out of a place of rejection, hoping people will like them because they are prophetic. I have seen prophets prophesy the party line to stay in favor with the pastor. Again, prophesying to win man's favor, or to please man, is a dangerous practice.

In Galatians 1:10, Paul wrote, "For do I now persuade men, or God? Or do I seek to please men? For if I still pleased men, I would not be a bondservant of Christ."

The other side of working to win the favor of man is the fear of man, which brings a snare. As one delivering a prophetic word, our goal is not to win man's favor but to please God with our obedience.

PROTOCOL 92
DON'T PROPHESY GENERIC WORDS

God is not generic, but too many prophetic words are. Generic means "having no particularly distinctive quality or application," according to *Merriam-Webster*'s dictionary.

Like generic drugs, generic prophecy is cheap. Although edification, exhortation and comfort may not be deeply detailed, generic prophecy takes on a different form in a social media age.

For example, we see a lot of prophecies on Facebook in particular that are vague or so generic and widely targeted that it's impossible to tell who it's really for. These prophecies usually start off with, "This is for someone..." and then promise some grand blessing or windfall.

What happens next? People are so desperate they are "claiming" the word as their own when God did not say it to them—and maybe never said it at all. Many wind up with deferred hope and a broken heart because that 24-hour windfall—or whatever they were claiming based on their interpretation of the generic word—didn't happen.

The other side of generic prophecies is they are so vague it would be hard to prove they actually came to pass. These are blanket prophecies the could literally be for everyone, but consider this: if a prophecy is that broad is it really prophecy? If it applies to everyone, do we really need a prophetic word to reveal it?

People need prophetic words that apply to their lives right now, not words that could be for everyone or no one. As prophets, we should press in and get more specific. At the same time, when prophesying personally over someone's life, I must repeat, sometimes the edification, exhortation and comfort is generic. But if it's for that person, it's for that person. It's not for everyone on social media.

PROTOCOL 93
DON'T CONTRADICT SCRIPTURE

The Word and the Spirit agree (see 1 John 5:8). Always. The Holy Spirit does not speak on His own but He speaks what He hears from Jesus (see John 16:13). Jesus said He and the Father are one (see John 10:30). Father, Son and Holy Spirit are in complete unity and the Trinity will never contradict itself.

Contradict means "to imply the opposite or a denial of," according to *Merriam-Webster*'s dictionary. Contradiction, or what I call prophetic Scripture-twisting, is a dimension of false prophets. You don't want to step into this dangerous dimension of Scripture-twisting even accidentally. This is why you need to be a student of the Word and a lover of the truth.

Some argue the Bible itself contradicts itself, but this is a lie of the enemy. Remember, the spirit of prophecy is the testimony of Jesus (see Revelation 19:10). If the prophetic word contradicts Scripture, it is not the testimony of Jesus because Jesus is the Word made flesh. The New Living Translation puts it this way, "For the essence of prophecy is to give a clear witness for Jesus." And the Good News Translation says, "For the truth that Jesus revealed is what inspires the prophets."

PROTOCOL 94
DON'T SCARE PEOPLE WITH YOUR PROPHECY

Don't prophesy words that are liable to scare the socks off people. God has not given us a spirit of fear, but of power, love and a sound mind (see 2 Timothy 1:7). There is no fear in love (see 1 John 4:18). In Romans 15:13, Paul describes God as a

God of hope. Even Isaiah, who prophesied judgment after judgment, is known as a prophet of hope. We are prisoners of hope (see Zechariah 9:12).

Some prophetic words may be wrapped in the spirit of the fear of the Lord (see Isaiah 11:3). That is much different than a spirit of fear. The spirit of the fear of the Lord is a holy fear rather than a demonic fear. Demonic fear has torment. The fear of the Lord is the beginning of wisdom to walk out the prophetic word.

A spirt of the fear of the Lord in the context of personal prophecy inspires us to reverence the Lord, to stand in awe of Him and His plans. The fear of the Lord inspires us to take the prophetic word seriously and to make any necessary changes in our lives in order to see the prophetic word come to pass. The spirit of the fear of the Lord helps us obey His leadership into the prophetic promise.

PROTOCOL 95
DON'T PLACE ENCOUNTERS ABOVE SCRIPTURE

Prophetic history has seen some ministers fall into the trap of placing spiritual encounters above Scripture, and even establishing doctrines based on encounters with God. This can be tempting after an intense spiritual encounter, but be careful. Paul warned in 2 Corinthians 11:14: "For Satan himself transforms himself into an angel of light." Anyone can be deceived, which is why we have to test the spirits (see 1 John 4:1).

One specific pitfall in prophetic ministry is indeed the overemphasis on messages from angels. Angels are messengers, and I believe angels can deliver prophetic messages and interact with prophets and other believers. But, again, we must test the spirits.

Paul warned in Colossians 2:18, "Let no one cheat you of your reward, taking delight in false humility and worship of angels, intruding into those things which he has not seen, vainly puffed up by his fleshly mind, and not holding fast to the Head, from whom all the body, nourished and knit together by joints and ligaments, grows with the increase that is from God."

Angels warned John the apostle, who walked with Christ Himself, not to be led into false worship through an encounter: Revelation 19:10 reads, "And I fell at his feet to worship him. But he said to me, 'See that you do not do that! I am your fellow servant, and of your brethren who have the testimony of Jesus. Worship God! For the testimony of Jesus is the spirit of prophecy.'"

It's not just encounters with angels that can lead us astray. We can have encounters with familiar spirits posing as God or family members. Judge the encounter and don't create theology out of your encounters. You can, rather, let your encounter back up Bible theology. Know the Word.

PROTOCOL 96
DO WALK IN LOVE

God is love, so everything He thinks, says and does is motivated by love. Because love is who God is, there is nothing He can do that contradicts love. As prophets, we must cultivate a fiery hot love walk as a matter of importance. No matter how accurate we are prophetically, we need to make walking in love a priority.

1 Corinthians 13:2 cuts right to the heart of the matter: "And though I have the gift of prophecy, and understand all mysteries and all knowledge, and though I have all faith, so that I could remove mountains, but have not love, I am nothing." Jesus said, ""By this all will know that you are My disciples, if you have love for one another" (John 13:35).

1 Corinthians 13:13 assures us, "And now abide faith, hope, love, these three; but the greatest of these is love." 1 Corinthians 16:14

admonishes: "Let all that you do be done with love." And Ephesians 5:1-2 encourages, "Therefore be imitators of God as dear children. And walk in love, as Christ also has loved us and given Himself for us, an offering and a sacrifice to God for a sweet-smelling aroma."

We know that: "Love suffers long and is kind; love does not envy; love does not parade itself, is not puffed up; does not behave rudely, does not seek its own, is not provoked, thinks no evil; does not rejoice in iniquity, but rejoices in the truth; bears all things, believes all things, hopes all things, endures all things. Love never fails. But whether there are prophecies, they will fail; whether there are tongues, they will cease; whether there is knowledge, it will vanish away" (1 Corinthians 13:4-8).

In my book, *The Making of a Prophet*, I wrote, "Love will also safeguard your calling. Think about it. If you are walking in love, you are going to be obedient. If you are walking in love, you aren't going to merchandise God's people. If you are walking in love, you are going to be humble. If you are walking in love you are going to be gentle. The fruit of the Spirit is going to manifest in your life alongside the spiritual gifts."

PROTOCOL 97
DO COMMIT TO EQUIPPING THE SAINTS

True prophets have an equipping mandate. Although emerging prophets may not be yet ready to teach others, mature prophets should be tapping into Ephesians 4:11-16:

"And He Himself gave some *to be* apostles, some prophets, some evangelists, and some pastors and teachers, for the equipping of the saints for the work of ministry, for the edifying of the body of Christ, till we all come to the unity of the faith and of the knowledge of the Son of God, to a perfect man, to the measure of the stature of the fullness of Christ; that we should no longer be children, tossed to and fro and carried about with every wind of doctrine, by the trickery of men, in the cunning craftiness of deceitful plotting, but, speaking the truth in love, may grow up in all things into Him who is the head—Christ— from whom the whole body, joined and knit together by what every joint supplies, according to the effective working by which every part does its share, causes growth of the body for the edifying of itself in love."

Some believe the primary function of a prophet is to prophesy. While I understand the concept, in truth the primary function is to equip believers. Of course a prophet is going to prophesy just like a dog is going to bark. But the primary function of a dog is not to bark. The primary function of a dog is to be a companion, or to help hunt, or to sniff out criminals. Yes, the dog barks as part of his function, but the dog was not created only to bark.

As a prophet matures and gets equipped himself, he should be actively looking to help others understand the voice of God and inspire in them a hunger for intimacy with God. This will make the Body of Christ less dependent on prophets for prophesy and help stem the tide of deception and the exploitation of believers from false prophets.

PROTOCOL 98
DO BE A PERSON OF PRAYER & INTERCESSION

There's a disturbing trend among some prophetic camps. Some prophets don't feel the need to pray. They will preach and prophesy, but prayer seems like a stranger to their closet. As a prophet or prophetic person, prayer is vital. Prayer is our lifeline to God. Personal intimacy is a must for prophetic people.

Did you know the first time we see the word prophet in the Bible, we see a direct connection to prayer? When King Abimelech took Abram's wife as his own, God visited him in a dream and told him he was a dead man for his deeds. Abimelech told God he had no idea she was married. God said:

"Yes, I know that you did this in the integrity of your heart. For I also withheld you from sinning against Me; therefore I did not let you touch her. Now therefore, restore the man's wife; for he is a prophet, and he will pray for you and you shall live. But if you do not restore her, know that you shall surely die, you and all who are yours" (Genesis 20:6-7).

Catch that: "he is a prophet, and he will pray for you." You can't separate prophets and prayer. This is not the only witness in Scripture we find to this truth. Jeremiah 27:18 says, "But if they are prophets, and if the word of the Lord is with them, let them now make intercession to the Lord of hosts, that the vessels which are left in the house of the Lord, in the house of the king of Judah, and at Jerusalem, do not go to Babylon.'"

The New Living Translation says: "If they really are prophets and speak the Lord's messages, let them pray to the Lord of Heaven's Armies." And the AMPC puts it this way, "But if they are true prophets and if the word of the Lord is really spoken by them, let them now make intercession to the Lord of hosts…"

Notice the use of the word "if." True prophets enjoy prayer and make intercession. It's part and parcel of the calling of a prophet. Some may have a heavier emphasis on intercession than others, but prayer and the prophetic go together. Cultivate a prayer life. It helps keep you steady and ultimately makes you more prophetic.

PROTOCOL 99
DO WORK ON YOUR CHARACTER ISSUES

Some believe that just because they can prophesy an accurate word, God doesn't mind their angry outbursts at home. Or because people are slain in the Spirit when they lay hands on them, God is pleased with the way they treat their friends. Or because a gift of healing is present, God is giving them a pass on that drinking problem, sexual sin or whatever else is hidden behind closed doors.

We need to be careful not to confuse gifts and callings with maturity and character. God can use a stubborn mule to prophesy, and he can use a stubborn believer to prophesy too. That doesn't mean God endorses stubbornness, which is like the sin of idolatry (see 1 Samuel 15:23). It just means that God needed a vessel to deliver the prophetic word to a person who desperately needed to hear it. That prophecy—or powerful altar call or gifts of healings or working of miracles—isn't about puffing up or glorifying the vessel. It's about edifying the church and glorifying God.

Good character doesn't earn you spiritual gifts and anointings, and poor character doesn't remove them, at least not overnight. By the inspiration of the Holy Spirit, Paul wrote, "For the gifts and the calling of God are irrevocable" (Romans 11:29). The Greek word for *gifts* in this verse is *charisma*, which means "a gift of grace, a gift involving grace" on the part of God as the donor. This verse is often applied to God's free grace to sinners, but I believe it can also apply to spiritual gifts and ministry callings.

If God called you into ministry, He isn't going to revoke that call or the gifts that go with it the first time (or even necessarily the 10th or 20th time) you act out or sin. Ultimately, it's we who turn our backs on our ministry when we repeatedly disobey God like Saul did. God is so slow to anger and abounding in mercy (Num. 14:18) that it may seem like we're getting away with our poor behavior and behind-the-scenes sin. God is just giving us space to repent.

We don't have to be perfect to prophesy a perfectly accurate word. We don't have to have a flawless character to minister at the altar. We don't need to be absolutely sinless to lay hands on the sick and see them recover. But we should work to cultivate Christ-likeness in our character. The highest calling we have is not to prophesy, but to yield to the process of transformation into the image of Christ.

PROTOCOL 100
DO CHECK YOUR PROPHETIC MINISTRY MOTIVES

Motives matter. As on fire and sold out to the will of the Lord as you may be right now, motives are something we have to check and keep in check as we continue in our prophetic ministries. Too many prophets have fallen to the lust of the eyes, the lust of the flesh and the pride of life because they didn't think they could or ever would (see John 2:16). But that prideful stance of not being willing to admit you could miss it with your motives can set you up for destruction.

The motive for engaging in prophetic ministry is to share the mind and will of God with people who need edification, exhortation, comfort, correction or direction. The motive, ultimately, is rooted in a love of God, in service to Him, and the love of people who need prophetic ministry and to be equipped to hear the voice of God.

Paul wrote, "Let nothing be done through selfish ambition or conceit, but in lowliness of mind let each esteem others better than himself" (Philippians 2:3). If you are engaging in prophetic ministry for any selfish ambition, such as to be seen, to be accepted, or to make name for yourself, your motivation is wrong.

Paul wrote, "And whatever you do in word or deed, do all in the name of the Lord Jesus, giving thanks to God the Father through Him" (Colossians 3:17) And again, "And whatever you do, do it heartily, as to the Lord and not to men" (Colossians 3:23). A good motive for prophetic ministry is to please the Lord by serving as His mouthpiece to help people.

Now and again, especially as opportunities come and your ministry grows, take the time to do a heart check. Remember Proverbs 21:2, "Every way of a man is right in his own eyes, but the Lord weighs the hearts." And again, Proverbs 16:2, "All the ways of a man are pure in his own eyes, but the Lord weighs the spirits."

If someone suggests your motives have strayed, don't automatically shut them down. Take some time with the Holy Spirit to pray. Remember Haggai 1:5, "Now therefore, thus says the Lord of hosts: "Consider your ways!" And in the Spirit-inspired words of Paul, "Examine yourselves as to whether you are in the faith. Test yourselves. Do you not know yourselves, that Jesus Christ is in you?—unless indeed you are disqualified" (2 Corinthians 13:5).

These following words—The Message translation of Jesus own words in Matthew 7:21-23—are sobering:

"Knowing the correct password—saying 'Master, Master,' for instance—isn't going to get you anywhere with me. What is required is serious obedience—doing what my Father wills. I can see it now—at the Final Judgment thousands strutting up to me and saying, 'Master, we preached the Message, we bashed the demons, our God-sponsored projects had everyone talking.' And do you know what I am going to say? 'You missed the boat. All you did was use me to make yourselves important. You don't impress me one bit. You're out of here.'"

PROTOCOL 101
DO RUN WITH A COMPANY OF PROPHETS

In the Old Testament, prophets ran together in companies, or schools. In the days of Samuel, Elijah and Elisha we see this concept repeatedly. The term "company of prophets" comes from the King James Version of the Bible.

1 Samuel 10:5, KJV, "After that thou shalt come to the hill of God, where is the garrison of the Philistines: and it shall come to pass, when thou art come thither to the city, that thou shalt meet a company of prophets coming down from the high place with a psaltery, and a tabret, and a pipe, and a harp, before them; and they shall prophesy."

1 Samuel 10:10, "And when they came thither to the hill, behold, a company of prophets met him; and the Spirit of God came upon him, and he prophesied among them."

1 Samuel 19:20, "And Saul sent messengers to take David: and when they saw the company of the prophets prophesying, and Samuel standing as appointed over them, the Spirit of God was upon the messengers of Saul, and they also prophesied."

There are many benefits of being part of a company of prophets. First, you are tapping into prophetic synergies. Second, when you hang around other prophets you create prophetic atmospheres. A rising tide lifts all boats. You'll find you become even more prophetic are prophetically sharper if you keep company with prophets.

Third, when you have other prophets in your camp you have people who understand your calling and the types of spiritual warfare and other challenges and opportunities you face. No one understands a prophet like another prophet. Fourth, you have other prophets to help you judge words, and to discuss prophetic concepts with.

If you are a prophet and you don't have other prophets you can turn to for wisdom, fellowship, and prayer, you are missing out on a key opportunity for personal growth. You can join my company of prophets and prophetic people at *www.ignitenow.org*.

ABOUT THE AUTHOR

JENNIFER LECLAIRE is an internationally recognized author, apostolic-prophetic voice to her generation, and conference speaker. She carries a reforming voice that inspires and challenges believers to pursue intimacy with God, cultivate their spiritual gifts and walk in the fullness of what God has called them to do. Jennifer is contending for awakening in the nations through intercession and spiritual warfare, strong apostolic preaching and practical prophetic teaching that equips the saints for the work of the ministry.

Jennifer is senior leader of Awakening House of Prayer in Fort Lauderdale, FL, founder of the Ignite Network and founder of the Awakening Blaze prayer movement.

Jennifer formerly served as the first-ever editor of *Charisma* magazine. Her work also appeared in a Charisma House book entitled *Understanding the Five-Fold Ministry* which offers a biblical study to uncover the true purpose for the fivefold ministry and *The Spiritual Warfare Bible*, which is designed to help you use the Bible to access the power of the Holy Spirit against demonic strongholds and activity. Some of Jennifer's work is also archived in the Flower Pentecostal Heritage Museum.

Jennifer is a prolific author who has written over 50 books, including

- *The Heart of the Prophetic*
- *A Prophet's Heart*
- *Fervent Faith*
- *Did the Spirit of God Say That?*
- *27 Keys to Judging Prophecy*
- *Breakthrough!*
- *Doubtless: Faith that Overcomes the World*

Some of her materials have been translated into Spanish and Korean.

Jennifer's other titles include:

- *The Spiritual Warrior's Guide to Defeating Jezebel*
- *Developing Faith for the Working of Miracles*
- *The Making of a Prophet*
- *Mornings with the Holy Spirit: Listening Daily to the Still Small Voice of God*
- *The Next Great Move of God*
- *An Appeal to Heaven for Spiritual Awakening.*

Beyond her frequent appearances on the Elijah List, Jennifer writes one of *Charisma*'s most popular prophetic columns, *The Plumb Line*, and frequently contributes to *Charisma*'s Prophetic Insight newsletter. Her media ministry includes her website; 500,000 followers on Facebook, Twitter and YouTube. Jennifer has been interviewed on numerous media outlets including USA Today, BBC, CBN, The Alan Colmes Show, Bill Martinez Live, Babbie's House, Atlanta Live and Sid Roth's *It's Supernatural*, as well as serving as an analyst for Rolling Thunder Productions on a *Duck Dynasty* special presentation.

Jennifer also sits on the media advisory board of the *Hispanic Israel Leadership Coalition*.

Jennifer is affiliated with:

- *Network Ekklessia International (NEI)*, an apostolic network founded by Dutch Sheets
- *Forerunner Ministries*, founded by Ken Malone
- Bill Hamon's *Christian International Network*
- Chuck Pierce's *Apostolic Network: The United States Coalition of Apostolic Leaders (*USCAL)
- *The International Society of Deliverance Ministers*

Jennifer has a powerful testimony of God's power to set the captives free and claim beauty for ashes. She shares her story with women who need to understand the love and grace of God in a lost and dying world. You can also learn more about Jennifer in this broadcast on Sid Roth's *It's Supernatural*.

OTHER BOOKS BY JENNIFER LECLAIRE

Angels on Assignment Again

Decoding Your Dreams

The Seer Dimensions

Seer Activations

Power Seers

Your Prayer Secret

Walking in Your Prophetic Destiny

Victory Decrees (devotional)

The Spiritual Warrior's Guide to Defeating Water Spirits

Releasing the Angels of Abundant Harvest

The Heart of the Prophetic

A Prophet's Heart

The Making of a Prophet

The Spiritual Warrior's Guide to Defeating Jezebel

Did the Spirit of God Say That?

Satan's Deadly Trio

Jezebel's Puppets

The Spiritual Warfare Battle Plan

Waging Prophetic Warfare

Dream Wild!

Faith Magnified

Fervent Faith

Breakthrough!

Mornings With the Holy Spirit

Evenings With the Holy Spirit

Revival Hubs Rising

The Next Great Move of God

Developing Faith for the Working of Miracles

You can download Jennifer's mobile apps by searching for "Jennifer LeClaire" in your app store and find Jennifer's podcasts on iTunes.

GET IGNITED! JOIN THE IGNITE NETWORK

I BELIEVE IN PROPHETIC MINISTRY with every fiber of my being, but we all know the prophetic movement has seen its successes and failures. With an end times army of prophets and prophetic people rising up according to Joel 2:28 and Acts 2:17-20, it's more important than ever that we equip the saints for the work of prophetic ministry. Enter Ignite.

Ignite is a prophetic network birthed out of an encounter with the Lord that set a fire in my hearts to raise up a generation of prophets and prophetic people who flow accurately, operate in integrity, and pursue God passionately. I am laboring to cultivate a family of apostolic and prophetic voices and companies of prophets in the nations who can edify, comfort and exhort each other as we contend for pure fire in the next great move of God. My vision for Ignite covers the spiritual, educational, relational and accountability needs of five-fold ministers and intercessory prayer leaders.

You can learn more at:
http://www.ignitenow.org.

THE AWAKENING PRAYER HUBS mission in any city is to draw a diverse group of intercessors who have one thing in common: to contend for the Lord's will in its city, state and nation.

The vision of Awakening Prayer Hubs prayer spokes is to unite intercessors in cities across the nations of the earth to cooperate with the Spirit of God to see the second half of 2 Chronicles 7:14 come to pass: "If My people, who are called by My name, will humble themselves and pray, and seek My face and turn from their wicked ways, then I will hear from heaven, and will forgive their sin and will heal their land."

For many years, intercessors have been repenting, praying, and seeking God for strategies. Awakening Prayer Hubs intercessors will press into see the land healed, souls saved, churches established, ministries launched, and other Spirit-driven initiatives. Blaze intercessors will help undergird other ministries in their city, partnering with them in prayer where intercession may be lacking. Although *Awakening Prayer Hubs* prayer spokes are not being planted to birth churches, it is possible that churches could spring up from these intercessory prayer cells if the Lord wills.

You can find out more about this prayer movement at:

http://www.awakeningprayerhubs.com

You can also join the Awakening House Church Movement at:

http://www.awakeninghouse.com

Or plant a house of prayer via Awakening House of Prayer at:

http://www.awakeninghouseofprayer.com/startahouseofprayer

CPSIA information can be obtained
at www.ICGtesting.com
Printed in the USA
LVHW020435050620
657404LV00021B/1182